Salvation

Salvation

By
GEORGE DOMAZETIS

Foreword by Andrew Bullen, SJ

RESOURCE *Publications* · Eugene, Oregon

SALVATION

Resource Publications
An Imprint of Wipf and Stock Publishers
199 W. 8th Ave., Suite 3
Eugene, OR 97401

www.wipfandstock.com

PAPERBACK ISBN: 979-8-3852-7372-0
HARDCOVER ISBN: 979-8-3852-7373-7
EBOOK ISBN: 979-8-3852-7374-4

VERSION NUMBER 040926

Bible sources

Nelson's Ultimate Bible Reference. Copyright © 2003 by Thomas Nelson Inc. Libronix Library System technology.

QuickVerse 10. Basic Edition. QuickVerse. Accessed at www.quickverse.com.

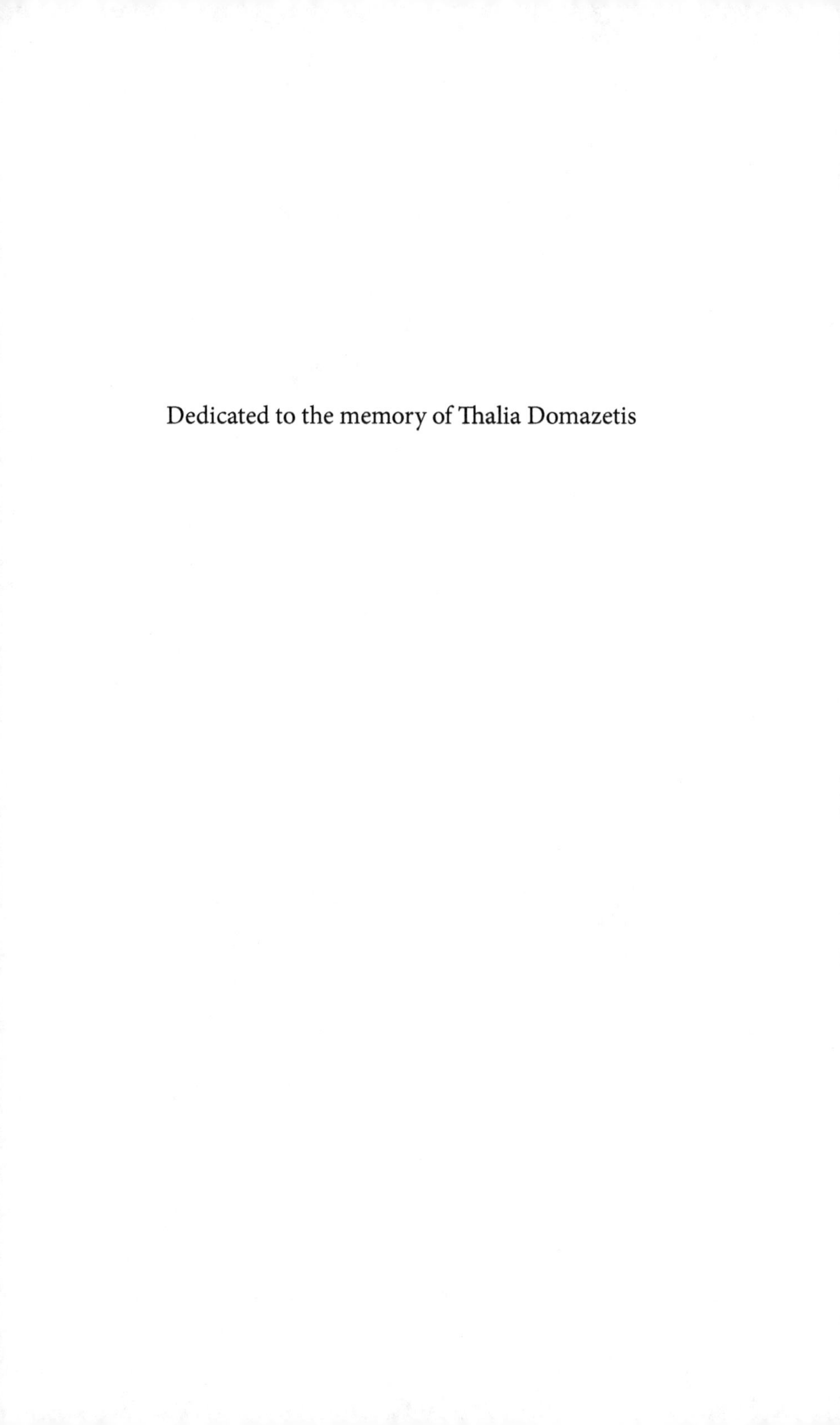

Dedicated to the memory of Thalia Domazetis

Contents

Foreword

George Domazetis' poem is an act of piety. He has deeply personal reasons for this. These private energies, however, have led him to reach out as far as one can. As a consequence, the scope of the poem is vast - it includes the universe, it tackles the human need to know that life has meaning and that such meaning is ultimately benign to us.

It is very unusual for poetry nowadays to encompass so much so directly; we are more used to poems that look like small fragments embodying a picture of a fragmented world. Here, however, a writer's personal desire to find the shape and scope of his universe has drawn on the potent orthodoxies of his religious tradition. The intellectual task has heartfelt energies.

The poem is also unusual because it is written by a person whose training is scientific. I know all too little about science, but I gather its stance now is more modest than it once was about how much of human life it can cope with. Maybe our imaginations are also less hidebound by presumptions of what can and cannot be done.

So this poem is unusual but welcome for another reason today - to put it bluntly, it's about God, and is so very directly. In presenting religious matters imaginatively, we can either be very indirect and "hidden" or be boldly grand about it. This poem, like Milton's "Paradise Lost" or the "Revelation of John" in the New Testament, takes the latter way. This is what makes it so interesting and challenging, and unusual.

But what really matters is to be moved by it. To experience this, we have to be alert as we read it to the drive and freshness of its language, to the effect it has on our imaginations, to what lingers within us afterwards - maybe indeed to have our own pieties stirred.

Andrew Bullen, SJ

Introduction

THE PURPOSE OF THE faith in Christ, the begotten Son of God, is the salvation of humanity from sin into eternal life in God. This is shown in the life, crucifixion, and resurrection of Christ.

This work endeavors to deal with the essential elements of the gospel and the faith that God grants to those He calls as an act of grace.

One may reflect on the meaning of such essential elements. I consider reflection on elements of faith as a personal choice, an act of freedom. In this brief introduction, I have outlined some matters that have formed the basis for my reflections, especially while writing the poem. I am a scientist familiar with the prevailing views on nature and the impact of scientific knowledge on modern culture, and my outlook is that science and faith are in harmony. These introductory remarks, however, are not presented as complete arguments or as theological treatise, and the poem is not based on a particular scientific view, or a systematic philosophy, or a synthesis for new ideas.[1] My hope is that the poem may show that reason increases because of faith in Christ and the goodness of God impacting on our way of life. However, we often seek meaning in life, and for a discussion on God, it is necessary to be able to attach meaning to that word. A discussion on the essential elements should begin with the question, "Can I state the word God in a meaningful way?"

1. The context is Orthodox theology, particularly as expounded in Patristic writings.

Knowledge and the Idea of God

What can we know of God? Ordinarily, what is comprehended is in the context of our awareness. Knowledge cannot be considered such, if we cannot be aware in some manner of what is being known. Christianity considers God as a being with attributes such as, for example, all-powerful, all-knowing, all-wise, eternal, unlimited by space and time, and so on. Yet it is not possible to point to anything that a human being may know or identify that would fit these attributes. One may point to the universe as infinite in some way, and be satisfied that such an attribute is known, without necessarily having direct knowledge of God. Meaning for a human being requires that it be within and part of the person, otherwise knowledge can only be of an object—such knowledge derives its meaning from sense responses to that object. If a human being cannot obtain meaning within self, speculation, and skepticism result. Meaning, however, may be attributed to an idea that would be intelligently constructed as an idea of God. This would be a synthesis of an idea, and the meaning is part of that idea.

The argument may be stated in another way. A human being can say God, and attribute additional words to the term, to be satisfied that the word has been used correctly in that language. Sensibly it is not possible to point to an object called God and then prove that the object is absolute, all-powerful, ever-present, and so on. It is sensible to note the practice of using the word god in our culture and consider a meaning as widely accepted. The historical context may be a starting point for the question, "Can I state the word God in a meaningful way?"

Historically meaning of various matters has been sought through metaphysics (nowadays also through a type of inner psychology or spirituality). It may be argued that the term god, has emerged over thousands of years as a synthesis of human imagination and then sustained through the circular usage of words (and for conceiving gods with human attributes, as for example in Greece and Rome). However, such methods cannot be considered valid since God in total meaning contradicts human synthesis. It is part of Christianity proper to view such a synthesis as insufficient.

It may appear that the term god cannot be used in a sensible way, and the question may not be answered adequately by philosophy. One may consider metaphysics for proof(s) of God as discussed, for example, by Kant who postulated the dialectic and the need for transcendental system(s). For this brief discussion, we note a negative response to the question, in that we cannot synthetically nor intuitively derive meaning and knowledge of God. The meaning cannot originate from a human being. Christianity proposes that the meaning of God has been received from people who testify to have used the word God in a way that has meaning to them. Their testimony is that God has revealed Himself to them.[2] The meaning that they communicate originates from God. This meaning cannot be derived in any manner from a human being, but it may be communicated amongst us—the meaning is communicated using words and symbols. The meaning is God Himself, since only He can be that meaning. Criticism may be made of this thesis because it removes an appeal to intellectual methodology by which meaning may be attached to words and presents epistemological (and perhaps ontological) problems regarding revelation. If we cannot appeal to philosophy and intellect, how can we know anything? We are characterized by the capacity for reason and knowledge. It is not my intention to argue against this. It is my intention, however, to argue that for the word God to be the meaning that we attribute to that word, we need to be capable of containing such a meaning within self. By appealing to revelation, we still require that we who are revealed unto, can comprehend such revelation within the possibilities of human beings.

When considered in a formal fashion, the meaning of God appears complicated, or to the skeptical mind contradictory. Intellectual honesty has often forced people to agree that there are many examples when god was created by man, and specifically desired meaning(s) attached to the term god for political (or other)

2. Revelation, for example, is discussed in "Dei Verbum: Dogmatic Constitution on Divine Revelation."

reasons. Yet when the Gospels, the Epistles of Paul, (and indeed the Bible) are read as a means of communicating beliefs on the matter of faith in Christ, formal logic, or scientific methodology of the time, was not utilized. Christ did not teach his disciples logic, nor did they appear to have undertaken philosophical debates. This suggests at least that although formalism may appear complicated, sensible discussions may take place.[3] Is philosophy inadequate for the task?

We note that Western and Eastern theologians labored with matters pertaining to the Godhead for many centuries, culminating in the Patristic writings and later works such as those of Aquinas and his proofs of (or five ways to) God's existence.[4] Briefly, western philosophy has developed over the centuries from Hellenistic roots, especially from the writings of Plato and Aristotle. Although theological discussions were not continuations of Hellenistic philosophy, certain aspects were considered close to the thinking of prominent theologians. The nature of such schemes appears to gravitate on the idea as the ultimate reality, and the categories providing the foundation of knowledge (understanding), particularly empirical knowledge. We may add that modern philosophy, such as Descartes' view, considers that after all is considered uncertain, the only certainty that a human being could obtain is in thought, which is taken to prove the existence of the essential nature. Additional arguments consider God's existence proved by, for example, being as the first cause of all effects, while God does not require a cause. The view of mind and matter was questioned by Spinoza who determined that there was only one substance which in its infinite one-ness is God, while all other beings are finite substance and individual. The interesting notion has also been put forward

3. The doctrine of the Trinity considers matters pertaining to God the Father, the Son, and the Holy Spirit, discussed in Patristic writings.

4. Theologians discuss apprehension of God as apophatic (*via* negation) and cataphatic (*via* affirmation). Apophaticism attempts to apprehend God by denying of him finite limitations, as He is indescribable and inconceivable by humanity. Cataphaticism affirms God by analogous likeness to created beings, thus using positive terminology, and may result in intellectual cognition, deduction, speculation.

that we may be considered as passive or active and that passion may be viewed within such a context. It may be inferred from this that freedom within a completely determined world is an act of will, by which the passive is transformed into an active being and through reason attain to freedom by which that being became part of the pre-determined world.

These scant remarks are directed at the question of human understanding of the meaning of God (and not a discussion of philosophical schools). While philosophical considerations have dwelt on the nature of being, at a glance, these do not appear to deal with the divine/sacred and the material/sinful world, nor is sufficient weight given to life as the basis for such considerations, although matters of the sacred, the material world of objects, and so on, are discussed by various writers.

We may surmise reason is faced with the dialectic which stems from dealing with the idea as central to reality (which cannot be proved) and this may lead to skepticism. Kant considers the ideal of pure reason as the ground for the ultimate idea, and to me, this may indicate reason is providing its ground; perhaps pure reason is speculative, but practical reason has a moral use, so the purpose of reason is freedom and happiness. The ideal of the supreme good is to provide the ground for reason to a moral world. Although this supreme good may be taken to mean God, I believe, instead, that such an outlook may be the idea of completeness and absoluteness of being thought to arise from reason.

Briefly, I posit that philosophy may have introduced a problem if Christianity accepted Plato's premise that the idea provides the ultimate reality, or an archetype. Such an idea originates from a human being (for the sake of argument, Plato is the originator, although the Greeks acknowledged many gods have a part to play). The major arguments developed by Western philosophy on the idea of God are often problematic, as metaphysics alone is unable to provide proofs for the existence of God and the soul. More recent developments have tended to separate philosophy and science from matters of faith, but arguments may be made that Christianity had been influenced by Hellenistic philosophy and may re-appear in modified forms in modern thinking. Thus, inspiration for the Poem is drawn from the Bible and elaborations in Orthodox Patristic writings and doctrinal matters of the Church.

The poem commences with a declaration which is cataphatic in that God is described using terms familiar to us; it is understood that we may necessarily (or intrinsically) respond to revelation by the grace of God. We are unique (in the Cosmos) in that we have the capacity to choose to respond, based on intent and will (e.g., created in the image of God; God breathed into man the breath of life). I propose that a human being within this context, may be stated as "life-awareness-self" (personhood). Within this view, all our knowledge revolves around life. Death is the cessation of life—as such death is the contradiction of knowledge. Reason arises from "life-self-awareness" and is subordinate to life. Reason is bound to the continuation of life. There is nothing beyond this, no ultimate end to reason. The completeness of an idea in reason is a product of reason and cannot be considered as completeness of "self-life-awareness." The completeness of a human being is found in the male-female relationship, as this is the means for the continuation of life. Our awareness and knowledge are based on life and ways that show it does not cease. The relationship of male-female is given added importance within the Christian context as it includes not only sexual attraction and romantic attachment but also: *"God has shed his love abroad in our hearts."* This provides a Godly basis for the continuation of life as it includes God's love in the male-female relationship. (The term "love" has very wide usage, including feelings of affection, endearment, and erotic impulses. The term is restricted here to the meaning of God, or synonymous with the Holy Spirit and fruits of the Spirit). As our sins are forgiven through Christ, knowledge of God becomes synonymous with life and the completeness of human beings. Those in Christ are abroad with God's love which is the basis for all things to life.

Knowledge as either empirical or abstract, and ideas which are the result of human intellect and reason, are of necessity part-and-parcel of actively engaged in the world of objects. Completeness of life, when considered as knowledge, is when death is removed as a reality of not-life to self. Life eternal is the life that comes from God through faith in Christ. Our life is finite because of sin and thus death is the end of a timeline. Death is not a thing that can be known. Christ is the way to life and by the forgiveness of sin, to life eternal. Arguments which attempt to prove or disprove the existence of God are in themselves futile. Denial of God and the meaning of the word are also futile, as the word god is used frequently, and discussion about god or gods is found universally.

It is sufficient for this introduction to show that knowledge of God cannot originate from us and thus arguments and various syntheses cannot provide the meaning of God. The meaning of God that we have is the result of God's revelation and grace. We perpetuate life *via* a husband-wife (male-female) relationship. The ultimate relationship is that which perpetuates life eternally *via* the relationship between us and God.

What then can be said of human knowledge, even if it is argued that this amounts to an awareness of self, the world of objects, archetypes, and myths? Awareness of self does away with the idea that knowledge is totally a brain-thing (as modern thinkers, we may note a distinction between consciousness and *self-consciousness*). However, difficulties arise when we entertain thoughts of, or about God, and thus think of the supernatural as distinct from the natural.

The poem begins with a declaration of God – but all terms used for this are of concepts, objects and similes that are found in common language. An additional requirement is that these terms cannot be such that we may construct an image of God. It is not possible to believe that we can think God in any manner. Only the Holy Spirit can know the things of God. I note that Christ, as the teacher to his disciples, asked them who they thought Christ was (i.e., Matt 16:17: Who do people say that the Son of Man is?. . . He said to them, but who do you say that I am? Simon Peter answered, you are the Messiah, the Son of the living God. And Jesus answered him, Blessed are you, Simon son of Jonah! For flesh and blood has not revealed this to you, but my Father in heaven). Christ himself is showing this cannot be taught in a classroom by a teacher, as in this example, all the other people who heard Christ (if this were a simple lesson) would have comprehended the teaching; yet even though Christ is the revelation itself, this understanding is by the grace of God who reveals this to us.

Classical theology discusses the essence of God and attribution of simplicity and impassibility. For this discussion, it is enough to point out the difficulties confronting notions relating the knowledge of God with our human comprehension and sense-based experiences. For example, the central theme of Christianity is that God gave his only begotten son to die an agonizing death, for a world that is separated from God because of sin. Yet our knowledge of God is that he is all powerful, holy, and just. Considered in this manner, it follows the central theme in Christianity is contradictory to our usual understanding and activities, because we cannot believe an all-powerful being would willingly allow his son to die, at the hands of sinners, who hate his son because of their perversity. This example illustrates the problem arising from conceptualized knowledge of God. Reason would dictate that a father with sufficient power would intervene and save his son from the actions of perverse people, and human experience shows that this is the case. But then, what of God? Is he less than human? Through this example, we may see the problem arising from the notion that God may be described by human attributes. It may cause us to question beliefs of the divine that we may acquire from daily experiences and intellectual endeavor. The paradox becomes especially serious when it occurs because human attributes are equated with godly attributes from our concepts and ethics.

Concerning God and the creation (general revelation), natural theology/philosophy has proposed views that: (1) God acted as He willed to gift the Universe and is actively engaged in the creation, and (2) God established immutable laws which are etched on all things, and He ensures these are maintained in the creation. Both views are interesting, but debates currently focus on the notion of laws of nature, which may become entangled with the Law of God. We may note that during the Middle Ages a sophisticated distinction existed between theology in the Christian sense and natural theology in the ancient Greek sense, even though some thinkers tried to unite theology and natural theology. Nowadays, we often observe a rejection of natural theology for philosophical and theological reasons (yet a revival of natural theology is noted amongst some sectors in an attempt to demonstrate the existence of God without relying on revelation).

For our purpose, it is enough to state the fact of God as Creator establishes a reality concerning the universe. The Faith teaches that God created all from nothing and he sustains all things (*creatio ex nihilo*). The Universe includes matter, energy, space and time; all are knowable to human beings (intelligibility of the universe). God is not subject to anything in His creation, and it is a gift. However, it is important to note that God is Sacred and Holy, while human beings are not. It is this separation between the holy and the sinful that underpins all discussions regarding human knowledge, including that of creation. The heavens declare the Glory of God; they do not chatter theorems and equations. Our capacity to know and conceive ideas related to the universe is a unique aspect that is re-enforced by the discovery of universal constants; however, knowledge of God is revealed.

Revelation and the Necessity of Faith

Theology discusses God and humanity and includes arguments that may be constructed (*via* speculative philosophy), on matters pertaining to conceptions of God. The following summary is typical: theology may deal with dogmatic ascertains, or may be natural theology, or consist of arguments about God. Such activities include wide ranging writings, such as on the Trinity, the incarnation, the making of man, and so on (e.g., ranging from Athanasius, Gregory of Nyssa, Aquinas, to the 20th-century theologians, such as Karl Barth). Theologians have endeavored to construct theology as a science that radically differed from the natural and the human sciences because its ultimate subject, God, was not accessible to empirical investigation. Barth considered God's freedom and revelation (communication of himself), as providing the understanding of God. In this way Barth believes one may avoid the danger of approaching God as an object of investigation.

When considering revelation, even if it is agreed that we avoid considering God as an object for empirical investigation, we cannot reason that revelation may be within a range of natural phenomena accessible to our human senses. We have ruled out objective-based activities such as found in the natural sciences. Revelation cannot be defined as a philosophy or a science that may be argued and tested experimentally. In making negative statements about our capabilities, I need to show that my arguments are reasonable; it is not necessary for an argument to be testable as absolutely true, but it is necessary for what is reasoned to be coherent and believably true. Those aspects of reason and knowledge that are intuitive (and indeed all knowledge), are usually subjected to tests of falsification (theoretical) and verification (practical) in the sciences, and to criteria of reason in philosophical discussion. It is my assertion that reason needs to sustain goodness and the continuation of life. It is possible for a person to consider the good in life through experience (*a posteriori*).

Regarding revelation, the person being revealed unto needs to understand, respond, reason, and to consider this within his/her (context of) life. The meaning of God, which includes that of love and concern for all humanity, is provided by revelation and needs to be completely comprehensible. Since I understand all human life and reason to be within the freedom of birth, of life, and of thought (intent), revelation is also understood within freedom. The unreasonable part of the human condition is lack of freedom that finds its ultimate condition in death.

Theologians discuss general and special revelation; for the present discussion, it is sufficient to note that we would respond spontaneously, instinctively, to revelation, and subsequently we may decide to consider and reason regarding the experience. This argument may be developed into a major premise that equates revelation of the meaning of God with the meaning of life (i.e., gives our life meaning). Briefly, such meaning is the goodness that God provides to life. This goodness is synonymous with the Holy

Spirit. Reason may respond to revelation rather than synthesize (or contrive) an idea of revelation. In general, I believe such a respond is *via* the ideal (not to be confused with idealism). Any reasonable person may respond to revelation in this manner. Some may communicate this ideal in almost illiterate ways, while others may communicate this ideal with great elegance. The response of reason, nonetheless, is of the same content, which can be summarized by the love that fills the heart, soul and mind of the person, in response to the revelation of God. The response of reason to revelation is thus life-giving. This includes the response to scripture as the Word of God, which provides an increased awareness of God and includes the goodness that results in life from God. Such a response is due to the Holy Spirit guiding reason rather than a scholastic analysis of words (such activity may occur afterwards). Freedom is the framework for the possibilities of goodness to reason on an individual level and on the social level (thus general possibilities). Revelation of God is not coerced, is founded within the goodness of life from God and is comprehended within such goodness.

It is part of objective reality, however, that communicated knowledge may also be considered as given and its origin comprehended. In the case of an awareness that arises as a response of reason to the revealed goodness, this can be considered as lawful, as principles, and the equivalent of verified knowledge (i.e., believably true). The finest example of this is the great law, of loving God with all the heart, mind and soul, and the second law, which is similar, in that we would love our neighbor as ourselves, which sum the Ten Commandments. These articulations (and the prophets, the gospels etc.,) are the eloquent wording of the ideal, the response of reason to the revelation of God, contain examples of the life-activities of those filled with the goodness that comes from God (culminating in the life of Jesus Christ) and are therefore wordings synonymous with the meaning of the word God. These remarks would also apply to our weakness and faults, in that the Bible would contain examples of these faults to teach us that God realizes our wrong choices and acts and wants us to be sufficiently self-aware to repent.

The goodness of life is within the completeness and the continuation of life. Revelation is presented to us within such goodness and revealed things become meaningful. Furthermore, because revelation is comprehended as goodness, it is in harmony with reason. The possibilities regarding revelation arise from the response of reason, in that each person may respond according to his reason and heart, and because revelation can be comprehended within the framework of life and death, within good and bad. Our reasoning shows that God is synonymous with good and life. Death is comprehended as either cessation of life, causing fear and anxiety, or death is equated with that which is contrary to God and is outside of the meaning of God. The remarks concerning the idea(s) of god(s) and the capacity for us to conceptualize such entities within the context of human attributes, provides many possibilities that reason may ponder and consider, providing error to the meaning of god. Because of the many possibilities that confront reason we recognize the necessity of faith.

At this point we may consider poetry as an appropriate medium for expression of faith (metaphor, simile, analogy); poetry is characterized by a quality of beauty and intensity of emotion. When writing the poem, words have been used in a way that meaning is found within the finiteness of human life but may also include (as an expression of hope and faith) the meaning of God as believed. This may be illustrated by considering the word, mercy:

Mercy—a meaningful term within the finitude of human life.

God is infinite—meaning is extended into an infinity which I cannot consider in a phrase such as "I am infinite" because this is meaningless to myself.

Mercy which may be comprehended within the finitude of human life, is now considered as endless and infinite, by the term "God's Mercy" (κύριε ἐλέησον). We comprehend this as God's will to be expressed for humanity *via* the doctrine of grace, as goodness from God. This is the way that we may obtain a coherent understanding. Words invoking God in various verses are not intended to ascribe human attributes to God, even though the concepts of mercy, grace and will, may be understood within human activity, as acts that enable us to proscribe a meaning that may be communicated between human beings. Without revelation and faith, the activities should be properly described as: (possibilities of) acts of mercy or cruelty; grace or brutality; will to good or will to evil. Human activity as such is found within this manifold. To make the phrase "God's Mercy" meaningful requires us to remove a good and evil duality, and to understand a singularly divine attribute relevant to the good of humanity. It is a Godly attribute revealed to humanity – its meaning can only originate from God (discussions of the Trinity, the essence of God and His revealed attributes are found in many theological writings).

Why discuss faith and science *via* poetry? Science is characterized by factual data and definition aimed at bringing a precise meaning *via* words and mathematics; often however, we note conflict, such as evolutionary notions of common descent over millions of years, opposed by advocates of descent of humanity from Adam and Eve over 6,000 years, and believing the age of the world is similar (creationism). Atheists often reject religion and some claim that it is a source of error and conflict. The general response(s) to such conflict is to point out that science is based on objective factual material, while faith is based on life-affirming experiences and thus subjective. Yet both seek the truth.

The necessity of faith becomes obvious. The singularity in the phrase "God's Mercy," rather than the human attribute of a plurality of, for example, mercy-cruelty, provides a one-ness to all God-related terms. We could continue to reason about God by associating additional terms which are normal to the human understanding, as for example, God may be merciful, and God may punish. When this reasoning is placed within a divine context, we attempt to rationalize that God may only punish justly, otherwise we would contradict our basic notion that God is total goodness. This is an attempt to incorporate what we regard normal, with good, and extend this to what we think is God-like. However, we would encounter more contradictions. We may re-consider our previous example, of God being all-powerful, but would not punish those who were committing a crime in killing his Son. As this would contradict our reasoning of how we think God should justly punish sinners, we would synthetically provide additional attributes of God to deal with the result of our own reasoning that has placed the meaning of God within a human context. In this case, our example may lead us to conclude that God is merciful to sinners and is a good god, since he can show mercy under circumstances that we cannot. If the term "God's Mercy" was reasoned as that, we would arrive at the meaning of God as more than human. That is to say, God may do things which transcend human capabilities, but such acts are within the possibilities of humans if they could rise above themselves (similar to a heroic view expounded in literature). The meaning of God is not that of a hero who has human attributes that we would admire and aspire to, but rather God saves us from the human attributes (works of the flesh) into attributes revealed by Jesus Christ, known to Christians as the works of the Holy Spirit.

Our consideration so far has moved from an overall problem stated initially as, (a) god is less than human, followed by, (b) god is more than human. Both statements are incorrect. We may say however, our understanding increases when meditating on the Godly attribute of mercy. It is not that the term becomes transcendental to us; mercy within a godly context is not contrasted to anything, and to us it is an attribute which may grow within life-self-awareness (our personhood). The notion of divine mercy is comprehended and consequently we grow within this divine attribute in our understanding and actions. This reasoning is extended to all attributes shown by Jesus Christ to us as Christians, and we grow as God's family (further discussion would be on Christ and kenosis). We also note that Christ was fully human and fully divine when He walked amongst us.

Faith is necessary because as human beings our life's outcomes are inevitably subjected to outcomes that are good and bad. We do not, however, need to experience evil to understand good; such a pernicious doctrine would be the source of a great deal of error. We have shown that life is good, and death is bad. Yet life is often filled with trouble and suffering. This is experienced and known through observation. Faith shows that God is the provider of goodness to life. The revelation of God and the faith in Christ require hope and security that the goodness of life can be attained and sustained in spite of the evils surrounding us. Faith would cause a person to appeal to God to provide the hope and anticipation that the attributes that are revealed by God would be within reason and life. Faith also provides the assurance of the completeness of life (God is life eternal) and the belief the finitude of life may be considered within this completeness (that God would forgive our sins). This is a very brief consideration of theodicy.

The faith from God teaches us to live at peace with God and with our neighbor. Faith is an essential element of the relationship between God and us, is illustrated in the male and female relationship (faith is life sustaining) and in a communal sense in the relationship between Christ and his Church. Faith is an essential element for the common good, for the community. Faith is the basis for the law that God provides for the common good, in that the community ultimately may have all things in common, since goodness can never vary. Faith is given (by the grace of God) as our sins are forgiven through repentance, a result of the sacrifice of Jesus Christ. The faith is in Christ, from Christ, since the sacrifice of Christ for us is acceptable to God the Father.

Community, Law of God, and Freedom.

Social interactions in a community, as people relating to each other (or identifying with each other), are initially an extension of the male-female relationship. A community initially consists of families, relatives, growing into tribes and ultimately through increasing populations into nations; interactions become increasingly complex and unstable, actualizing into structured systems, such as for example, a class system. Such systems may attempt to achieve stability through the creation of power centers, but these often increase the complexity of the community, with conflicts resulting in crime, war, and destruction.

It is within such a communal problematical we may appeal to law, and a brief discussion is thus required on the notion of law. Such a discussion, however, cannot be carried out without consideration of freedom. It is assumed that we have a capacity for choice to act in some manner, and this will be discussed within our understanding of the notion of law. A brief comment may be made on the anthropological view regarding communities and civilizations. A great deal of speculation exists on how life may have begun and the origins of humans, with records of civilizations that have risen and fallen over various periods during the last 10,000–60,000 years. A historic/anthropological view introduces a cultural aspect to this discussion; for brevity the phrase "essential elements" is used here to differentiate from cultural matters. A discussion on the distinction between "essential elements" and "cultural matters" is outside the scope of this introduction. It is nonetheless sufficient to recognize that human activity consists of essential matters pertaining to human life and the well-being of all life on earth. History shows communities grow, and cultural diversity is an outcome of such growth. It is also recognized that civilizations have embraced, in some manner, the notion of law.

There are three generally accepted meanings for the term law: (1) a rule or system of rules recognized by a country or community as regulating the actions of its members and enforced by the imposition of penalties; (2) a statement deduced from observation, to the effect that a particular natural or scientific phenomenon always occurs if certain conditions are present; (3) the body of divine commandments as expressed in the Bible (or other religious texts); the law according to Moses provides commandments that are summarized in Deut 6:5 (love of God) and Lev 19:18 (love your neighbor as yourself), and the Gospel perfects these by the teachings of Christ.

The term law may thus refer to legislative law, scientific law, and the law of God. The first phrase refers to a legal statement introduced by a community and is enforced within the community.

The second phrase may be considered as intrinsic to an object that ensures our observations of the object and its dynamic properties are so in time and space. The third phrase needs to be discussed within revelation and the meaning of God.

(1) *Legislative law:* Laws of modern communities emanate from binding agreements, usually termed the constitution of the nation, or compact by the members of a community to be subject to their rule of law. Communities create institutions to legislate and enforce specific laws. In this case individuals of that community may choose to accept that law and consequently modify their behavior in some way to conform to that law; conversely, they may not accept a particular law through choice or may regard it is in their interest not to submit to that law. Each person in the community makes a choice due to his/her disposition, and the resulting behavior could be judged as obedient or disobedient of that law. A judgement in terms of obedience or disobedience of a law would be based on specific facts and acts that have been witnessed by members of the community, and the factual matters may be re-enforced by a confession from the perpetrator. The community authorizes agents to enforce such laws or rules and makes known the enforced consequences for disobedience of the law.

Legislation would show how the community has recognized the problematic and acknowledged the need for all its members to make a choice to conform to legislated law in that the common good is served. It is possible, however, for problems to continue even if, hypothetically, the community chose to conform completely to such law, because the legislation may be faulty. The basis for such law is derived from the community that has endorsed its social compact; the nature of the compact would be based on a collective understanding by the community, particularly of the various activities that it believes would produce non-beneficial outcomes. Although the attitude may be one of endeavoring to find the common good for the community, historically this has been a platitude, and such law was an attempt to deal with the problematic emanating from power struggles, and as a result such law may be a means of perpetuating the problematic within a community, rather than solving it.

(2) *Scientific law*: This is generally understood as laws of nature and includes outcomes to the human senses (and to reason) from nature's activities, or phenomena—these responses may be quantified by observation and hypothesis and tend to suggest an instrumentalist attribute of a human being in a world of objects. I would argue against instrumentalism, but I believe a non-passionate view, as an indifferent response to nature, is reasonable as this is ultimately based on material facts. Observations and hypothesis by scientists are activities of our reasoning in that we measure, weigh, calculate etc. We are active in thinking and measuring, and these activities are within nature. In this way activities are of matter and energy in time and space, (in motion or in a dynamic state) and considered explicable *via* the scientific method. It is erroneous to believe that we bring a law into existence when providing a theory, a hypothesis, or a formulation. The difficulty faced by us is that of differentiating between ourselves as reasoning beings, and the objects of our inquiry—since both appear to be the world. This actualizes into language activity, which leads to a differentiation between the world of phenomenon/dynamics and that of human reality which seeks explications in time and space by the scientific method.

If nature's laws are known, a person's actions and anticipated consequences should be explicable, but may not necessarily be changed through choice. The dynamics of any natural system would be the same whether these were, or were not understood, even if one conforms to such dynamics. Science attempts to provide explanations or descriptions believed to encompass the universe. A law as something that may be considered as arising from reason applied to an object is unnecessary. It may appear, however, that mega-knowledge is sought to enable us to attain a complete understanding of the phenomena and its objects, and this may provide an intellectual perception, or inference, that objects behave according to some principle or objects are required to be as they are by something within them. This search for an explanation of everything, or a universal, arises from our intellectual questioning and doubting.[5] We may reason that the universe is lawful in some way, and we may eventually completely understand it. Such an outlook may seek comfort from an ideal, suggesting that the universe and our understanding of it will finally be totally reasonable. Instead, the essential question in natural studies is the intelligibility of nature – how is it that our intellect can access natural phenomena and realities? One response to this question is the attribute conferred to humanity by the image of God when He created all.

It has been suggested we may see the mind of God in the universe, but our previous discussion of the meaning of the word God negates such a view. The impact of the vast universe on our senses, however, may be overwhelming, as we seek to understand it. The universe does talk to us of God in its silence as shown in Ps 19:1–14. The writer of this psalm shows us that it is the law of God that he understands, and through the law of God, he hopes to be free from error and those that indulge in error. The universe does not directly reveal God, but it may point to its Creator (Rom 1:19–23). Our senses may be influenced by the silence, and our reason may comprehend the glory of God that the heaven declares. In this way we may understand beauty without feeling it is there because we have invented it. In this silence, we do not listen to our own feverish mind constantly trying to explain to ourselves all that our senses may respond. Rather, the glory of God proclaimed by the silent beauty may lead us to wish we could share, and be a part of, such splendor. The Universe in all its splendor points to its Creator's glory, and similarly to the beauty that is found in the law of God.

Currently astrophysics consider the origins of the universe. The difficulties of evolutionism are sidestepped by the notion that the universe is anthropomorphic—i.e., a universe that evolved conducive to the evolution of life and human beings. The origins of the universe are often discussed as the big-bang theory, although

5. An interesting discussion is by Tanev, *Energy in Orthodox Theology and Physics.*

other speculations can be found. Generally, the theological view has been that God is the cause of causes, or the primal cause; since no-one witnessed the event, we cannot discuss this notion as a verifiable/testable theory. It is necessary, however, to believe that scientists are interested in obtaining a good understanding of the universe. The scientific method requires theory to be tested—in this case, tests are performed using particle accelerators to obtain data on the particles that constitute the universe. These tests provide experimental data, and the methods rest on theory devised by physicists and are mathematical expressions that encapsulate the thinking of physicists and mathematicians. Furthermore, such experiments may be reproduced by other scientists, and theory may be examined, and increased understanding would result.

The limitations of language have been mentioned when considering the meaning "God" and concluded that all godly attributes are singular (doctrine of divine simplicity) and human language was insufficient to give full meaning. The universe, however, is accessible to our senses, and it appears reasonable to assume that a language such as mathematics would be sufficient when examining the universe. Difficulties are encountered, however, in that the origin of the universe cannot be quantified using the laws of physics, i.e., we contemplate notions of beginning in which the laws of physics may not apply. Indeed, notions such as "nothing existed before a beginning" are difficult ones for science to define *per se*.

Quantum physics generally commences with a mathematical equation to describe a system. We cannot be above the world, in a privileged position that transcends the universe, and analyze beginnings and ends of the totality of what can be known. The scientific method does enable us, however, to examine physical reality in the universe and dispassionately draw conclusions from our observations. If physicists conclude the wave equation may be expressed as the sum of the forces in the universe and these are measured in some way, then in theory such an activity conforms to the scientific method. If astronomers observe galaxies that provide light that has travelled for an enormous amount of time, and from this obtain an age for the universe, this too is reasonable (it may be inferred that postulating such an age includes a beginning). However, if scientists perform mathematical calculations and conclude that these observations lead to errors that are so large that under ordinary circumstances such results, according to the scientific method, must be considered speculative (e.g., cannot account for most of the calculated universe). Otherwise, we have the situation found so repugnant to scientists, in that irrational dogma replaces reason in the physical sciences. These scant remarks serve to indicate the limitations of the physical sciences, and the laws/theories of these sciences are relevant only to physical reality accessible to our intellect.

(3) *The law of God*: Strictly speaking, this cannot be understood empirically as a law God has placed in nature and derived from our study, nor as a law legislated within an assembly set up by God, nor one physically legislated by God that He forces the community to obey. Communities with a religious inclination and/or history may endeavor to encompass the law of God within legislative law. This usually arises because the community intends to base legislative law on what it thinks is the law of God. The articulation and communication of this meaning would be within the context of human activity. The law of God is stated as a command, but this is based on the overall command, to love God with all of one's strength. In the case of legislative law, a person obeys or else is prosecuted. The law, as articulated by Moses, can be understood as legislation, such as do not kill, do not bear false witness. But the law *in toto* is understood as the expression by Moses of the revealed will of God to Israel, and through Christ to all humanity.

The law as an expression of God's will would be total and would be synonymous with the Love of God. Scripture shows that the law would ultimately be written in the hearts and minds of God's people (Jer 31:31, John 1:17) through the grace and truth from Jesus. The gospel contains commandments from Christ which teaches and guides the Christian way of life. Sin is also understood as breaking the law of God (thus, salvation is by the grace of God).

If the law of God is comprehended as active concepts accepted by us based on, or because of, intent to love God, intention and act need to be considered. A separation of intent and act would introduce a possibility of an act actualizing differently to the intent. For the requirement of a one-ness of intent and act, an additional attribute is required from us, that of being lawful. If we were to erroneously assume the scientific view of law, such an attribute would require an intrinsic aspect of lawfulness within us, i.e., we would be an object in nature and that would negate intentional choice.

The Gospel teaches us that all have sinned and have come short of the glory of God. In practice humans have performed acts which are the negation of a lawful attribute. Some activity may also be understood within a judgement that shows an intent differed from the act, and such a result is comprehended as error (e.g., a person unintentionally killed another human). Judgement of various acts may encounter further complications, such as for example, if the intent of a person was to harm another person, and then he tries to cover this by denying that intent, he would be uttering a falsehood, and so on. The attribute of a person who intended and acted correctly (non-harm) would be lawful. We may also consider activity in which a person would not intend, nor act, to harm another person, and yet other factors lead to harm occurring (an examination of unforeseen factors would be warranted). Consequently, it is not possible to use the scientific method to identify a lawful attribute as intrinsic to humanity. We observe behavior and outcomes and seek to relate these to intent and personhood of the human being.

This argument enables us to recognize the capacity to display an attribute which may be lawful, and/or unlawful, based on choice, intent, act, and judgment. We are characterized, or comprehended, through our acts, and these may be judged within intent and actualization of that intent as shown by the facts pertaining to the act. Additional extraneous causes may also be considered in our judgement.

The belief that the revealed will of God is understood as the law expounded by Christ, enables the Christian to grow in the attribute of lawfulness (which is also a communal attribute since such activity impacts on other people). The command to love God, is the gift from God's Holy Spirit. This has been discussed above as goodness to us at a fundamental level (life-self-awareness). God has given us His Spirit and is stating that it is necessary for us to live within His Spirit—we also need to live amongst other people within His Spirit. By responding to God within total goodness, each person comprehends goodness from God to humanity, and in a like manner, we respond to other people within such goodness. This response is at the level of life-self-awareness and as such is intrinsic to self, and synonymous with the revealed goodness. The Holy Spirit reveals God's goodness.

This discussion may now be expanded; legislative law is required when people interact in ways that are potentially non-beneficial to some person(s). In cases where evil laws are enforced, the complexity within a community may be considered within the secular extremes of nihilism or totalitarianism. When religion is used to enforce such ideologies, these are labelled as fundamentalism, (dead/hypocritical orthodoxy) or regimented religious practices (institutionalization of religion by the state).

The problematical in a community would culminate in destructive acts or crimes. There are examples of people not of the faith who have appropriated the religious vocation to achieve personal ends. The dynamics of systems or structures populated by such people are understood as attempts to acquire power over others. For example, dictators may impose order to unstable communities, while the dictators themselves may be malevolent and are often insanely destructive. In religious institutions, external signs of piety may be observed, but internally they may be riddled with vice and perversity. It is clear, therefore, that the attribute of lawfulness is a requirement for a community to deal with such problems, and this attribute may be achieved through a free choice to obey the law of God.

The intent of a person needs to be based on a free choice regarding the law of God, and this requires the understanding that arises within the spontaneous response of reason to the revealed goodness. The aspect of law as consequences, in this context, is understood because of the beneficial outcomes to the community when people equate good intention with good action. The law of God as articulated provides the specific understanding of how particular good acts can provide good outcomes; it may also be specifically understood as the absence of benefits to people if intent and/or act are contrary to the law (by extension contrary to the revealed good). The law of God can thus be understood in the context of benefits to a community. It is also understood within the context of the absence of benefits and the potential for the community to sink into acts that bring misfortune. This again requires conscious choice and active effort on the part of the community. The law of God does not require enforcement; rather the community needs to choose to exist within the context of a collective lawful attribute.

The law of God deals with God-man (singular) and God-community (general). As discussed below, freedom is an essential element and stems from comprehending humanity as truly human within reason and freedom. The dynamics of human reality include changes in time within concepts of past, present, and future (past may be a memory, while communities formalize this as history). We understand our individual timeline as the period between birth and death. This may be considered an internal time that we contemplate as we render our life comprehensible; we may also consider an external time that enables us to understand the world of activity and objects, and our knowledge includes experiences as past and present, with continuation as it will-be, in our anticipated future. The time for the world is part of the explicable, in that our intellect comprehends the changes in space as dynamics or phenomena, but we require an additional concept to comprehend the world as continuing. I think that it is difficult to derive time from the world, and indeed we derive this as a measurement from periodic motion and subscribe a length of a physical movement to the notion of time. The derivation of our time as internal includes how we understand our existence and experiences (discussions on time are provided by various philosophers).

These scant remarks are indicative of the eternal, or atemporal, nature of the law of God as we consider doctrines such as original sin and grace, within this non-temporal notion. The law of God cannot be broken and, if we acted accordingly, it provides a practical solution to the problems arising from the complexity of communal interactions. The simplest practical statement in this context is, they have all things in common. A way the law of God removes the complexity/problematic is by enabling individuals to exist within a community through acts of service and patriotic sentiment; such individuals are part of the community seeking guidance by the Spirit of God regarding the active aspects of community interactions. All individuals comprising the community consider the collective well-being, and within a lawful collective attribute, decide on the application of commandments, principles, and rules in the same way they do in their individual actions. Difficulties can arise, however, when some people within such a community may not be guided by the concern of the general well-fare, and some may also choose to act in a malevolent way towards the community. It is within this context that the detailed articulations by Moses can be comprehended as "do not."

The law of God talks of God-mankind in the same way as it does of mankind-mankind. It is a common saying that a community needs to be within the spirit of the law of God for collective benefits to actualize. These benefits are concomitant with the development of the attribute of lawfulness to each member of that community, and a collective lawful outlook within the community. The law is also articulated, or is presented to a community, as the letter of the law. This is a practical proposition, and may, but need not by necessity, be legislation. When the law of God is applied in this way within a community, it is often in details which address practical matters that impact on the community (e.g., rest on the Sabbath, do not steal from people, do not kill people, and so on). This active, or practical aspect, is legitimate when the activities of people originate, or are motivated, from the goodness of God within personhood. It is in this way that an inviolate aspect to the law of God may be noted. This also indicates that instead of enforcement, it requires conscious choice by people to obey the law of God.

In cases where the intent of that community is not to conform to the spirit of the law of God, but rather to use the law of God to invoke authority over people, the attribute of lawfulness is usually not developed, and difficulties rather than benefits result—even though that community appears to include the law of God within legislation. This also implies an inviolate aspect to the law of God. Even when specified requirements of the law of God appear to be met, the results to people may be non-beneficial. This appears problematic when viewed from the perspective of scientific law, which indicates that consequences are set whatever the intention of people may be. It also appears problematic from the perspective of legislative law, as in this case, obeying the letter of the law is sufficient. The law of God is provided for a communal purpose, to form the basis for a collective outlook of the members of the community. It is in this way that a collective intrinsic aspect of the law of God is evident within freedom. Conversely, an ineffectual collective outlook towards God by the community results in ineffectual outcomes to the community. The law of God is an expression of God's will for the community. The law of God is therefore intrinsic to communal life, universally valid, inviolate, and sacred. The laws of science are articulations intended to deal with nature, while legislative laws result from difficulties experienced by communities. The law of God is initially a religious utterance, in that people, individually and collectively, are admonished to worship the one true God. The law of God also states that the love for one's neighbor is like the love for God. God does not take on the role of an agent for the community and police the law. Passively, the law may be obeyed through intent and spiritual inclination. Actively the law empowers a person in guiding his actions, and indeed, empowers the collective attributes of the community to bring about beneficial collective activity. The law of God is not understood as a definition found in a scientific law because outcomes are not determined until a choice is made by people in their intent and in their actions towards God and the community (the determined aspect is that we make choices and are able to understand what is good and evil).

The law of God may be considered all-encompassing as through it the attribute of collective lawfulness is created (the sermon on the mount shows this, Matt 5:1–48). Stated in another way, a community would live in a world in which all actions would lead to beneficial consequences and every act in the world would be within the law of God. The Christian faith is that Christ is a person whose intent and actions were completely within the law of God, but the world was not sufficiently determined in its actions and could not know that Christ is the Son of God. The world can be considered at fault, but its sin may be forgiven (as Christ stated, they do not know what they are doing).

Lawfulness and freedom at an individual level indicate a person may anticipate a range of possibilities that encompass the outcomes of his acts on himself and on the people of his community. Within a social context, a human being would consider a range of possible acts and understand that these may lead to further activity amongst people. The person would complete the social context in such a way that he/she may be within the activities that he/she wishes to initiate (all such activities originate from that person who may know if his actions were in accordance with the law of God). Since the person's actions impact on others (they may respond, and this would constitute further activity) all individual activities need to be according to the law of God in the social context (the community). It follows from this that for such a community, its activities must be in accordance with the law of God—thus a collective attribute of lawfulness is a logical outcome and includes freedom. Freedom is the ground for all acts and at this point in the discussion, it is sufficient to note it is an essential element in considering the possibilities of communal existence within the complexity noted above.

It follows that practical morality form within a lawful community. Morality is all that pertains to the well-being of human beings and to the world in which they exist.[6] Such morality is pointed to individual activity in the social context. The results from acts based on this morality are good for the individual, consistent with the completeness of life in the male-female relationship and are beneficial to other people. We can consider the individual within the context of all other people forming his/her community. The specificity found in the Bible regarding the law of God (e.g., do not kill, do not commit adultery, and so on) is provided to teach the practicality that is part and parcel of the law of God. We may conclude that the law of God is total and absolute because it: (a) addresses self-awareness *via* the attribute of lawfulness based on free choice, (b) addresses the complexity inherent in a community by providing the commonality of the individual and the collective, *via* the attribute of lawfulness, in that it includes a one-ness in intent and act towards others, and (c) provides the required practicality needed for a community to continually learn to be lawful through a collective morality that is comprehensible.

The social context, however, needs to be understood with humanities propensity to err (error is acting contrary to the law and will of God). To avoid error, a person must provide himself with a range of possibilities of action that are all-encompassing, with all outcomes beneficial to him and to others. This requires an absolute understanding of acts and all consequences. In practice, the comprehension of a person may be incomplete, thus providing the possibility of error; the choice may not be perfect, thus adding to the possibility of error; the final choice, or judgement, may be imperfect, providing further possibility of error to the prediction, and to the actualization of the act. On this basis, it may be impossible to conform to the law, in that he/she does unto others (perfectly for their complete well-being) on the basis that he/she may wish them to (perfectly, for complete well-being) do unto him/her.

Legislative law is the result of activities and judgements made over time by members of the community and introduced through

6. 1Cor 13:13, Gal 5:14–25

the governmental structure of the community. The law of God is a *law of God, from God, for humanity* and acts on people *via* understanding and choice. It cannot be anyone else's law, nor can it be a statement of phenomena, natural or otherwise.

An intrinsic aspect of the law of God may be difficult to contemplate because freedom is always in that way of life. It is accepted that all have sinned, and this is a negative statement to show us the importance of the grace of God. Even in communities that have legislated laws considered to be consistent with the law of God, the problem of sin cannot be removed. A community benefits from the lawfulness resulting from the intent to implement the will of God, and such intent and action are within freedom and faith. The will of God encompasses all things, including all notions understood as law, be these laws of nature, or legislated laws of a community. God's will be for the complete well-being and happiness of humanity, and this requires the exclusion of sin. The fact that unhappiness, suffering, and death are found in the world makes it necessary to remove the cause of these things, which is sin, brought by the author of sin, the devil, and removed by the sacrifice of Jesus Christ. The law of God is so sacred, inviolate, and necessary for the salvation of humanity from sin, that the Son of God sacrificed his life to provide the forgiveness of our sins.

Even though Satan is the author of sin, it is nonetheless sin committed by mankind. In the poem, the fall of Satan is described as a transformation of a being through his own will, and this transformation is initially passive, commencing with pride and vanity (Lucifer conceives himself as being greater, or other than what he is). The transformation is completed through an act, or force of will (war with other angels) involving the community of angels. This analogy is intended to show that a created being's will, freedom, and choice, impacts on his community. The destructive aspects are now considered to arise from a passive state, in that a being is capable of reasoning contrary to God's will, and from an active state, in that a being would use his reason to plan and execute actions that he knows will bring harm to others. The intent is known to such a person, and this transforms him into a lawless creature; this is an attribute that can also form within us if we now follow the path set by Satan. The attribute of lawfulness is developed by following in the footsteps of Jesus Christ and requires intent (to repent or turn away from sin) and an act of will; our action is motivated by love for God and similarly to others. Our intentions arise from a desire to do good as the individual and the community. This completeness of both intent and act for goodness within a person and to the community is the basis of all good things held in common.

Faith and grace are central for salvation. The intent to lawfulness is a pre-requisite and enables a sinner to reject sin, by recognizing that this is malevolence both in act and intent towards himself and others; this rejection (repentance) of sin also includes intent and act (will) to live his life according to the law of God.

In that a person is repentant of his sin, he is totally aware of the effects of sin on the individual and his community. Even though within an individual goodness may not be found because of the effects of sin, the faith that results, or is a gift, from God's Holy Spirit, causes a rebirth of the person through a re-awareness of the goodness in the divine nature and the capacity for reason to respond to that revealed goodness once again.[7] The power of sin (death) is no longer within the person because both the intent and action of the repentant sinner are now to life. Death is defeated by repentance and the faith in Christ—this is shown by (the act of) baptism in the death of Christ, and the resurrection (into life) in Christ, because life is granted by God. The salvation of that soul is an act (grace) of God and is possible through faith in Christ because that faith has resulted from the crucifixion of Christ as a sacrifice for our sins, a perfect sacrifice in God's sight. Faith is granted to us through the grace of God.

Freedom: I have mentioned freedom when reflecting on the essential elements of salvation. A distinction is made here between freedom as part of human reality, and the freedom enjoyed when humanity is with God (until then humanity is a slave to sin).

7. The doctrine of theosis.

There is extensive literature that deals with the various views on freedom, and in-depth discussion on this requires extensive reading and consideration of the many opinions expounded in writings over many centuries (beyond the scope of this Introduction). Freedom is often a term that encapsulates self-determination, autonomy, and unconstrained or spontaneity of a rational human being, including the absence of submissiveness and servility. The subject is all encompassing as the concept may be considered as an abstract and normative value of human action, or as a concrete experience of humans. It may be inferred that freedom within a completely determined world would be an act of will, so that a passive person is transformed into an active one through reason, and in this way attain freedom. An act of will may be consistent with choice, but the inference in this view is that freedom is considered within a completely determined world. Such a view is difficult to reconcile with choice, change, chance, and uncertainty found in the world (particularly that of human choice and the ability to interfere with other people's activity, and to interfere with natural activity). Does this mean that freedom cannot be equated with a human capacity to choose? And what can we say concerning human will!

Reflecting on the elements of faith is an act of freedom; thus, I have inferred that freedom is all pervasive when discussing salvation. I have in mind individual rationalities required for choice, and a collective or social freedom based on the communal response to the divine Law as a command to love your neighbor.

Theologians have noted that freedom includes the capacity to decide to turn to God, or to turn away from God, and such autonomy does not exhaust the choices available to us. These discussions need to be applicable to all humans in any circumstance e.g., those with medical/physical infirmities that may severely inhibit activity, healthy active individuals, various cultures, and those in various relationships. At this point of the discussion, we may use the following terms as fundamental to humanity:

"Awareness-self"—(I am, but I may exist with inhibiting infirmities) . . .

"Awareness-self-life"—(I exist as an active human) . . .

"Awareness-self-life-as-one"—(I am perpetuating life in a male-female relationship, in life-goodness, I worship within life-eternal goodness-revelation).

Our reality is understood within the plurality of our attributes as displayed by our activities (emotionally, intellectually, and physically). The term "attributes" is that which is understood within intent and identical in act—thus an attribute is identical in a passive *I am* and in an active *awareness-self-life*. The attribute is the same for a person actively displaying that act and to another who witnesses that particular action. The plurality of human attributes provides a range of possibilities and introduces uncertainty; this denies a totally pre-determined world to human reality. It also recognizes the capacity for error, which in religious terminology is the capacity to sin causing separation of human beings from the one-ness of Godly attributes.

The thesis in this discussion is that we (life-self-awareness) are in the world (not of the world, nor as emerging consciousness). Our reality is faced with chance, possibilities, and outcomes that are often such that we would wish to choose otherwise, after a conscious choice has been made. Additionally, even though we were to believe we had made the correct choice, the outcome may be contrary to what we initially understood should have been. The causality we believed was correct, may in fact prove otherwise for that act, resulting in an illusion of choosing correctly, but actualizing as "other-than-" the intended choice. Indeed, we are subject to the necessity of seeking the distinction between good and evil, which is accompanied with the bitterness of choice, highlighting the biblical teaching that we are slaves to sin, and all having sinned and come short of the glory of God (Rom 7:14–20).

When comprehending errors, we may confer regret or a judgement of self, after such an experience—this judgement of self may be self-reflective grounded on freedom; to reflect on the intent and act even after a choice and act have actualized in the world. This freedom has brought an acceptance (or responsibility) for the result, even though we may have concluded we had not intended what actualized, i.e., we may regret the deed, may question the intent, reflect on the nature of his intent, or conclude that we were ignorant of the resulting act, even though we initially believed that we understood the matter (or we may conclude the act may have occurred accidentally). Conversely, when intent, choice, and act are correct, and error is not observed, a judgement of self occurs to reflect on a one-ness of intent and act (and such is understood as good within freedom); additionally, we may also know what may have been otherwise. In this way, life-self-awareness as active, experiences freedom within repentance and the revealed goodness, or: life-self-awareness as active may experience an act (a) within a judgement of error, (b) a decision that we may wish to change from error, and (b) as a particular now judged to be true. Finally, a person who intentionally acted with evil intent may also conclude that the intent actualized in the act and judges his evil act accordingly as desired.

These brief remarks are valid if a person acts. While an intent and an act are required, in the case where a person is incapacitated, he may entertain intent, but cannot regret or affirm an outcome, nor an experience, since he cannot arrive at a judgement of a goodness/correctness of an act. However, our terminology is such that intent and act are required; (it is possible to consider a totally evil act to provide a one-ness, but this requires an absolute contradiction). A discussion on freedom thus needs to encompass human reality within a world in which correct and lawful outcomes, (what are observably correct), or erroneous, unlawful, and sinful outcomes (observably so) are possibilities confronting us.

In the previous section, enforcement of legislative law was noted regarding action, as this was a matter of a person's disposition. An apparent absolute or intrinsic aspect of natural law was noted; such a law was not subject to any choice or determination by a human being, but the correctness of the use of the term law, in this context was questioned, as science understands, and indeed believes, that objects are so in time and space, and a scientific law is an articulation of this understanding (which is often subject to error). While an intrinsic aspect of the law of God was also discussed, this was shown to be within the possibilities (outcomes) intrinsic to the law of God (i.e., outcomes are always understood as either good or as sinful). Even though enforcement of the law of God is shown to be unnecessary, freedom may appear problematic when any inviolate aspect is considered.

Freedom is often spoken as "the spirit of freedom"; a person's spirit may, or may not, be chained, or conditioned to evil, and it may also be committed to good. The essential belief is that life is given or created by God and in this way, freedom is inevitable—or when God created life, He created freedom in the same act, so that life, freedom, and the spirit of man are all encompassing. This infers that a meaning of freedom would be obtained from the revelations to the saints of God.

Freedom, however, is also discussed and intellectually comprehended by us; thus, freedom is argued by some to mean an absence of all constraints, often espoused by anarchists. A god-like freedom is sometimes considered as a being who is beyond constrains/consequences, above good and evil. These invoke, or assume, the totally powerful being has freedom to exercise all desires and can ensure that any act of will on his part is realized in whatever manner he chooses, or fancies. This god-like attitude may be embraced by unsound minds and is often an indication of insanity.

Freedom may be equated as the liberty to create a setting in which we may act according to our desires, wishes, and beliefs, while accepting various limitations.

Theological debates abound on outcomes that are considered pre-determined, with a causal chain resting on the primal cause of God the Creator; based on this argument, some conclude that since God created all, He also created sin and evil. Thus, such erroneous reasoning concludes that freedom and human agency may be illusions.

God created all as a setting for us as free agents to choose to live according to God's will, or to reject God. Ultimately, we would be cut off from God if we choose to, but even then, God grants us forgiveness as an act of grace. A determined quality is understood in that a soul can respond to revealed goodness; this is because God is the Creator. This does not mean that God may be bound in any way; God is not bound to reveal goodness to anyone, nor is he bound to a success rate of a positive response, nor is he bound to a promise, nor is he bound to a competition for souls. Thus, it is reasonable to conclude that salvation is *by the grace of God*. The response to the revelation is also *according to the will* of a human being. The response by Christ when he said, "God's will be done," is a response of total freedom.

When a person responds to the revelation of God as an expression of that person's will and volition, reasoning is such that his belief is total. Such a totality is often considered a commitment, and others may witness such commitment as with all of the heart, mind, and soul. The response is intrinsic and analogous to sensible responses in the world, such as to phenomena as facts and experiences in the world, with the exception that revelation is subjective. The response to revelation is also comprehensible as the spontaneity of reason arising from self to provide the instant, or the moment. This too is analogous to responding intelligently in the world. A similar response may be contemplated in a relationship (male/female), as it is in the one-ness and totality of being. Finally, a person who is incapacitated may passively and spontaneously response through reason to revelation.

This in no way implies that a personal experience of revelation would encapsulate God's goodness as a totality of God, or in some way the person has all knowledge *in toto*. The essence of God is not knowable to humans. Indeed, the person's understanding is according to his upbringing, education, abilities, and capacity to choose, to act, including his proclivity to choose either good or evil. A human's knowledge of what is good or otherwise is incomplete and consequently human reality is not changed spontaneously into a perfect or idyllic state because of the revelation. Choice and activity, the resulting consequences, and human attributes, remain. As a result, freedom is comprehended in human reality within the context of self-in-truth. He can only choose good by believing within himself that the act, intent, and choice he made is true, and consequently, believed as good (this is understood as acting in good faith). In truth, freedom as the ground for personhood (life-self-awareness) is comprehensible as far as it is his true self. This statement must necessarily be general, that it is applicable to a person in religious activities who communes with God, as created in the likeness or image of God, as one active in his community and caught up in day-to-day activities (religious or non-religious).

In falsehood, however, the person becomes "other-than-" or diminished. That freedom encapsulates, and is the ground for the exercise of abilities, involving intent, act, and self-comprehension, means that by intentionally undertaking false acts, a person actualizes as other-than-self. In practical terms, such a false-self is understood as consequential psychic states; these remarks are also valid to a community, and to the male-female relationship. These psychic states are pathological, and on a fundamental level, are attributes of personhood that have resulted from intent and act understood within the good-evil plurality of our attributes, such as cruelty or mercy, love or hate, and so on. The intent and act of cruelty, for example, by a human being will result in the active formation (for brevity, we use the use the term formation) of that sadistic attribute.

Likewise, the active intent and act of mercy will result in the growth of this attribute. A religiously disposed person may comprehend these as godly attributes and understand the growth as a deeper understanding of meaning from God. A non-religious person, however, may articulate such matters as beneficial and contributing to the common good, consistent with the attribute of lawfulness, whatever his private beliefs.

The destructive attributes of humanity have resulted in the destruction of the world. Creative and beneficial attributes, however, have made an addition to the world of beauty and to the well-being of humanity. For example, historical data shows destruction of ecosystems and species due to human activities; conversely data shows people have undertaken activities to ensure harmonious growth of ecosystems. Thus, if we live in harmony with the earth's ecology, the planet and humanity would flourish. The earth does not choose destruction—this is a human choice. Some acts of nature may be considered destructive to populations, such as earthquakes and hurricanes; such acts do not diminish the earth and perhaps we may find ways to avoid or minimize the impact on us of these events. People of a particular sensibility search for natural justice and a sociologically natural form of existence and only take from the earth what they need to sustain them and add to the earth to sustain it. Although such sensitivities are admirable, we cannot escape from ourselves or the problems that are part and parcel of humanity living within our various choices of good and evil.

We may express a passion for freedom. However, it is not sufficient for a person to feel that he/she is free, or to be aware of the world within a sense of freedom. It is that the human being is free. Stated another way, freedom is the completeness of being without any false-self (or self-deceit). Deceit-of-self is a contradiction through an act of will by that person—the act of will is such that the reasoning is altered. Freedom includes good and truthful faith. Freedom, within a spirit of deceit, or of evil, or bad faith, is not negated, but the person is actualized as other-than- (we may argue a form of negation, but this is un-necessary for the brief discussion here). From this we can deduce that freedom as actualized within, and as comprehended, is self-in-truth, while a will that consciously chooses deceit, chooses to exist as—other-than-(true)-self. This statement is also relevant in a collective sense—a community is free in the same way that singular units (persons) are free. A contradiction cannot be found in freedom and as the discussion on the law and the community has shown, a person acts towards God as he acts towards others.

The notion of self-deceit requires examination. Such a notion is more than entertaining what is fictitious. Deceit is most often a contradiction of what a self knows or believes is true. Such a person provides for himself, often for the purpose of providing to another intentionally, with a contradiction of what he believes is true. His intention and hope are to create a false description to other human beings. Strictly speaking, an untruth cannot properly exist unless it is completely synthesized as such, and in the world of objects this is impossible; fictitious works obtain their material from the world of experience and objects. Uttering a lie is bearing false witness in that a version of an event or a description differs from the event, or the object. In such a case, fact is sufficient to destroy the lie, and the false witness may be exposed by the fact. The truth of the object (or the factual description) may be found and has not ceased to exist, and it is understood that the fact existed, while the falseness is a contradiction of the fact. However, the act of falsification, or the falsehood (for the duration of that activity) diminishes the sense and reason of the one creating the falsehood, and to those who will continue to receive, believe, or accept, such falsehood.

A synthetic untruth, or self-deceit *in toto*, would involve the human intellect, sense, reason, and emotion. The act and the person are considered for that moment to be one and the same. Strictly speaking, a totally false thing cannot exist. Should a (complete) untruth be synthesized, it may assume aspects of factuality, and is thus believed by such persons, but it may not be possible for other human beings to discover this, as such a thing cannot be contradicted, or tested and falsified. Human reality generally is comprehensible as being and not-being; all statements, experiences, and thoughts may be questioned, and belief can be suspended for these activities. For a synthetic untruth or falsehood to be presented to reason as such requires it to be singularly so and not contrasted to something in any way. This is only possible if life-self-awareness were to be completely altered. (Mythically it may be viewed as possessed by demons). For a synthetic untruth, the person's identity would be annihilated, replaced by a "not-self/-other." This may be fictionalized as a destruction of the "true-self" followed by a creation of a "false-self"—however, a religious meaning of such things is the soul has died *in toto*.

Based on this argument, we would conclude that a human being can be a "non/other than-self," and such contemplation in the world, would amount to death, and we regard this as spiritual death. Generally, exercising of our will in this way would lead to a complex "true-false/self-entity." These may be understood as psychopathological disorders and have been shown, in many cases, to be the result of many factors, including physio-chemical disorders and is these cases, the disorders cannot be traced purely to willful intent and act *in toto*.

The attribute of lawfulness includes truthfulness and so a problem cannot be found when regarding law and freedom for an individual or a group.

Within normal (non-pathological) activities it is reasonable to comprehend an untruth as a contradiction of something. Science can be said to have freed humans from the lie of a fictitious world of material objects, by showing that a factual description is sufficient. The example of a world that is factually round, rather than the world is flat, illustrates this point. In this case, the world at no time became flat, but always remained round. The belief that the world was flat was widespread. This did not come about because someone knew that the world was round and conspired to deceive humans into believing that it was flat. Rather, it was truly believed to be flat. The loss to the freedom of human beings can be understood because of such a belief; they lost the freedom to explore the world for fear of falling off the edge of the earth. It is also interesting to note that some believed the world was round; nonetheless, some people thought it madness for anyone to travel too far as they could fall off the edge of the world.

If we accept an incorrect or false belief, we are constrained by the false belief. For example, idolatry is considered by those who believe it to be an act of worship. The idols are constructed objects, and the act of idolatry confers a belief of "other-than-" (the objects are a carved stone or wood) to an object (believed to be a god). This is complex because the fact the object is a specific material is verified sensibly, and thus a contradiction of that fact has not taken place. The act of worship of a god, however, is false. This belief needs to be sustained in some manner, since any reasonable person can understand the factuality of the material object (the person would not claim that the idol is in fact anything other than the material, such as stone or wood). The belief of such a person is of an object, and indulging in the act provides a meaning to the person *via* the belief the idol is a god, and this belief and intellectual outlook cannot be sustained without the idol and associated activity. The person is in a contradiction, and he has endeavored to alleviate the problem resulting from that contradiction, by means of an intellectual object – in this case the belief and worship are presented to such a person as true *via* an elaborate belief/intellectual structure that is designed for that purpose (thus an intent is imbedded in the belief). The purpose of idolatry is to provide a falsehood by conditioning the worshipper *via* act, belief, intellect, and intent. This form of conditioning, within an elaborate intellectual and social structure, in the extreme may result in the synthesis of an-other/false-self. Idolatry has been used to enslave people; in ancient cultures, history indicates some social/religious systems included human sacrifices, believing such acts pleased their gods and the community displayed the highest good. The pathological condition can lead to other-than-hope, other-than-faith, and so on. The other-than singular/contradictory attributes are the result of the contradiction imposed by reason and will on the soul; the practicality of such systems is fragmentation of self into subjective/objective aspects constantly posited on the object of false worship.

We may assume that several notions would appear as truisms to people who are individuated by an external power to believe such, even when these could be shown to be falsehoods. This cannot be taken to mean that in such cases freedom has been falsified or has been lost—it is that the soul may be lost, and it would experience a rebirth when finding the truth, accompanied by many changes. Such experiences would be accompanied by a deep desire for honesty; this change, or conversion, includes the growth of the attribute of lawfulness. Conversion and the resulting lawful activities may impact on ideas and views of the world but not necessarily include the skepticism associated with intellectual speculation. Repentance and a commitment to avoid sin may at times be taken by cynics to lead to a restricted understanding of the world of objects and phenomena—this is not the case. For example, the scientific method may require the suspension of judgement when gathering data and testing a hypothesis. As a scientist, I ascribe to a skeptical view, or exercising doubt, when considering physical reality based on the observation of physical and intellectual objects. I view doubt as a necessary ingredient in the pursuit of a factually correct description of physical objects as the scientific method includes theoretical considerations, with emphasis on testing and verification with standards and experiments. The scientific method is a major achievement because it includes testing theory, acceptance of aspects that have been verified, and doubt what could be falsified. All theory (and intellectual speculation) requires doubt and questions, but it is underpinned by the hope that it will eventually provide a factually correct, or at least, a reasonable description of the universe. This activity stems from hope and desire by human beings to search and find what is true of things and includes a commitment to ethics. Scientific endeavor, however, cannot examine spiritual matters and questions on revelation and faith (ethics deal with the integrity of the science methodology). One response may be to delineate between the good and not good and consider evil as the absence (or privation) of good. Human reality may also be considered as logical and sensible. Logic requires considerable education; the sensible aspect, however, requires a conscious choice to consider all human reality within a personal context, such as for example, that things are good, unless shown to be not good, and thus avoid attributing evil to the sensible world.

The teachings of Moses, crystallizing in the ten commandments, are that of not doing, e.g., do not lie, do not steal, and so on. Yet to identify an act as that which should not be done requires that a person can identify a good act. The apostle Paul states that when the law came, we began to comprehend the good from the evil of our acts, and yet this comprehension resulted in the knowledge that we chose evil acts. Does this mean that the law is evil? Of course not! Paul shows the human spirit would, if truth were to be its goal, die because the law has shown our falsehoods and evil acts; however, the revelation of Christ brings the resurrection and life: thus "I die as a result of sin (the act of doing evil), and yet I live in Christ (the result of repentance, faith and the resurrection)."

Paul also states: For what human being knows what is truly human except the human spirit that is within? (1 Cor 2:11–15) Those who are spiritual (according to Christ) discern all things, and they are themselves subject to no one else's scrutiny.

The person of faith who hopes for and seeks truth in freedom, accepts the source that empowers within freedom. This is a radical departure from the usual concept of power that is understood as power over others and over nature. It also differs from the popular notion of the exercise of power as authorized functions carried out within a community, as these are often corrupted into power over people.

We are also communal in spirit. It is the spirit of humanity that is capable of truth and of deceit, the spirit of kindness and the spirit of cruelty, capable of reason and sense, and loss of reason and resulting insanity. This duality/plurality of human existence stems from the loss of that spiritual state of Adam and Eve who originally communed with God in freedom as taught in Genesis and is the primary cause for suffering to humanity and to the world. The loss is the effect of sin and manifests as the contradictions of human existence; we may exercise good sense, show kindness and compassion—yet we can also show bad sense, be cruel, harsh, and destructive, as demonstrated in our acts.

The human spirit and the carnal human condition can desire freedom but can never be free from deceit; we are incapable of freely (and independently, without empowerment and help from God) to be truthfully the human being created in the image of God. It is the Spirit of God that can bring the human spirit into a life of freedom and truth. In religious terms, this is because of the love of God shed abroad in our hearts and takes place because Jesus Christ, the Son of God, destroyed death and ensured that life cannot be contradicted. As Paul states:

> But he that is spiritual judgeth all things, and he himself is judged of no man. For who hath known the mind of the LORD, that he should instruct him? But we have the mind of Christ.[8]

8. 1Cor 2:15–16

Faith and freedom are from God as a gift by the Spirit of God. The practicality of Christianity is understood in this way; for example, even though civilization institutionalized Christianity, and then contrary to the law of God, exerted authority over people in the name of Christ—even this great contradiction could not extinguish freedom from the human spirit. Freedom is found within the meaning of the name of Christ and prevents those who would endeavor to use it to enslave others. Freedom of the human spirit is also expressed through desire and passion, often resulting in noble deeds performed by individuals, and by communities, who glimpse the bright vision of freedom, and seek to live in attainable truth, rather than excessive deceit. Freedom is also found in the world of objects through art and science, in that a human being comprehends objects in a sensible and factual way and seeks to express these intellectually and as beauty.

The discussion is of freedom and spirit; it is important to understand that the term spirit is not used to indicate a non-physical supernatural being, nor an energy in a higher level of existence. We may speak of the human spirit as equated with human attributes, it is also equated with life, or the breath of life, along with terms such as spirit of truth, the spirit of freedom, intelligence, self-awareness, volition, i.e., the human spirit is equated with identity/personhood.

Freedom in totality is the truth of God, and we are totally free when we discern God (the beatific vision). It is therefore reasonable to conclude that freedom is the singular attribute concerning our experiences, our response to revealed matters, the exercise of our intellect and spirituality.

The teachings of faith are presented within the bounds of human comprehension, and the singular attribute freedom is the basis for this. This point may be illustrated by considering the mythical story of the fall of Lucifer; this posits that a created being contradicted God and subsequently transformed into falsehood and evil. It is understood that God is all-powerful, and thus a positive view cannot be intelligently sustained in this story if it implied a created being would have the capability to challenge and contradict God. We may deal with this difficulty by providing a setting, as in the poem, which presents angelic beings within a created framework of Heaven and the Universe. Yet a scientific statement would require us to synthetically provide a meaning that would overcome our incapacity regarding spiritual beings, since our sense-based knowledge requires a materialist setting. We discuss many non-material aspects of our existence, such as hope, faith, intellect, intent, etc., and these have been treated over the centuries using various genres. In this work I use poetry.

I have (arbitrarily) stated that a synthetic untruth or a total falsehood presented to reason must be singularly so and not contrasted to something in any way. This is ordinarily not possible, but I speculate that if a person (life-self-awareness) were altered into "other-than" this would be the meaning of a synthetic falsehood within the spirit of falsehood. In contradicting factual knowledge, we do not necessarily loose ourselves completely to freedom; we would develop the attribute of falsehood and would be on the wrong path, so to speak. However, if the human spirit were united, as it were, to the spirit of falsehood (considered the singular falsehood), and that person would be lost to freedom and transformed into a synthetic falseness. The story of the fall of Lucifer shows he was transformed into other-than, re-named Satan, the adversary who became the origin of sin. This change has its origin in a being created in freedom, but this is comprehensible to us by considering such a being (compared to that originally created by God), re-synthesized by his own will into Satan. A detailed discussion of these matters is the subject of theodicy and the controversy regarding universal salvation, or annihilationism, and will not be considered further in this Introduction.

Salvation: Christ on Earth, Christ Crucified, and Christ Resurrected

The Gospel urges repentance, for the Kingdom of God is at hand. It unambiguously states that all who repent and seek forgiveness, by the grace of God, will become citizens of the Kingdom. The central question to humanity is that of sin and redemption, the forgiveness of our sins through the blood of Christ and the growth of repentant souls into the children of God. This may now be discussed within the context of the first Adam and the last Adam. The sum of (good) human possibilities are comprehended, culminating in Christ; humanity progresses (its destiny) into persons who are like Christ. We may progress from our present state (symbolized by the first Adam) into that revealed by the actions and teachings of Christ (the final Adam). The works of the flesh are contrasted with the fruits of the Spirit (Gal 5:16–24), and Paul shows that we are inheritors of grace and are free when we grow in these attributes.

This thesis would require a careful review of the attributes of humanity as we are now, and how we attain to the ultimate attributes revealed by Christ. Overall, it is not a Miltonian view of Christ outwitting or beating the Devil, nor a Dantean view of a cosmological order into which people act to a result according to our human understanding of good and evil that ultimately actualizes into a hell for the wicked, a heaven for the blessed, and a purgatory for those in between.

In Part II, Book Three, the lines:

"My spirit beheld over centuries of time
Mankind progressing against the oppressor. . ."

. . . . refer to progression, and survival, against the intent of the oppressor (and subsequent verses show how we fail to avoid sin by ignoring the instructions of the law). Those Christians who are overly concerned with Darwinian evolution may be inclined to view the progress in these lines within their notion of evolution (or unfolding within time and space).

We may contrast these lines on progression with the erroneous view that institutionalized Christianity is a historically significant event, but anachronistic, a "dated movement." Of the factors responsible for this view, the prominent ones are materialism/physicalism, and Darwinism which has given added impetus to materialism. The Church has faced many challenges, internally ones requiring responses such as found in the Patristic writings, and external ones from pagans and state permitted persecutions (ultimately Christianity was adopted as the religion of the Roman Empire, rendering the Church an institution of the State which sought to subsume the Christian faith and to become a lever in the State's exercise of power). It is enlightening to read of accounts of the growth of the faith, in which similarities may be observed between the period of early Christianity and today. In earlier times, many groups declared themselves to be Christian but were in fact sects with social-political agendas. Today, the political situation includes many institutions with religious inclinations endeavoring to play a social/pastoral role politically. In this way, they espouse certain Christian principles of service to the community. Yet the situation today may be summarized by Augustine, reflecting that many people who wished to attend the church of that day may not have been of the Christian faith.

The subject of salvation is humanity progressing to become Christ like, and this encompasses all our hopes and aspirations. This universality renders salvation essential, and easy to understand with the background of human suffering over centuries; however, some are dismissive in that all of us hope for peace and wellbeing and such generalizations appear vacuous as they face the practical day-to-day difficulties of life.

The Apostles were called by God to be faithful witness to the truth concerned Christ as he lived, was crucified, and resurrected from the dead. The birth of Christ is discussed, for example, by St. Athanasius (On the Incarnation) and Gregory of Nyssen in his Dogmatic Treatises, where he expounds the meaning of the terms "Only Begotten," and "First born":

> . . . because we are by birth flesh and blood, as the Scripture saith, "He who for our sakes was born among us and was partaker of flesh and blood," purposing to change us from corruption to incorruption by the birth from above, the birth by water and the Spirit, Himself led the way in this birth, drawing down upon the water, by His own baptism, the Holy Spirit; so that in all things He became the first-born of those who are spiritually born again, and gave the name of brethren to those who partook in a birth like to His own by water and the Spirit. But since

> it was also meet that He should implant in our nature the power of rising again from the dead, He becomes the "first-fruits of them that slept" and the "first-born from the dead."[9]

Christ was fully human and fully divine. The genealogy of Christ commenced from Adam. In every way, Christ lived as a human being, with the exception that he was without sin. Christ was also fully divine, from conception to resurrection, yet he came as a servant (Phil 2:7) and chose to exist as one of us.

The image of Christ on the cross has symbolized Christianity for 2000 years and is a mystery that communicates the central tenant of the faith. Yet some may view this as a symbol of a great tragedy, in that Christ was sent to the chosen people, the tribes of Israel, as prophesied; Christ was rejected by the chosen people he came to save and was instead brutally killed and treated as the lowest criminal. Others take another extreme view, in that Christ rejected and crucified by the Jews is not only symbolic of the depravity of human beings, but also how pagans who lived in abysmal darkness and idolatry were now granted the very salvation so eagerly sought by generations of devout people of Israel who kept faith with God, often through great suffering. Such views are incorrect.

The cross is the common method of execution used by the Romans in that period. It cannot be given any other meaning than an instrument of death, and Christ died because this is the way people were executed in His day.

Christ died on the cross to defeat death by His resurrection.

Christ came to forgive our sins, for the conversion of human beings dead because of sin, now alive in Christ with godly attributes. This is a practical proposition. Salvation is, and can only be, an act of grace from God. We as finite humans would aspire to a godly life, with sin and death removed, resulting in God's eternal life at the final judgement. The question of an afterlife is now a godly life without death—that is eternal life. Salvation is the change or conversion into people with godly attributes, as the children of God, through baptism into the death of Christ, and

9. Gregory of Nyssa, *Dogmatic Treatises*, 215.

resurrection into life in Christ. The final change takes place at the last trumpet, or last day, and is determined by God.

Our thesis on human life and our exercise of reason means that there cannot be some other essence or entity to a human being. This does not mean that we are without a soul, rather soul is the person. The dependence on God is obvious since He provides eternal life. The view that salvation cannot be earned by acts, nor provided by the law, but is through the grace of God, becomes sensible within this context. If a human being contained some type of immortal entity, the question of death and life ceases to be of any concern. The end-result is simply the position that one may adopt in relation to endless activity. Reincarnation would be the option for a so-called immortal entity, rather than salvation. An immortal entity, once it has sinned, cannot be changed into a sin-less soul. Indeed, any change brought about by any act from, or to, an indestructible, immortal substance, appears difficult to understand, since the indestructible and immortal would lack a capacity to change. It is sufficient to recognize the spirit of humanity created by God cannot exist on its own volition, nor is it self-created and self-sustaining.

Questions may arise regarding universal salvation—for example, if all the attributes that accord to the one-ness of God are beneficial, why doesn't humanity access them now? Why should God show favor, so to speak, and choose to be gracious to some? If God is truth and mercy, He should have converted all of humanity by now and thus we would all live in a perfect world without the suffering and misery found on this earth. In this way, we transfer responsibility for our actions to God by virtue of the basic tenant of Salvation, which is that God saves humanity from death or sin, into life and goodness; the problems of theodicy remain however, in that we may question who made evil? The brief response is evil is activity chosen by an agent. Salvation is an act of grace by God, not an act of force, otherwise we would not have a say in repenting our sinful attributes and intentionally choose the Good. The Christian message is the Son of God came to live amongst us and although none could find fault with Him, we (or those who interacted with Christ) decided to put Him to death. This profound message shows that God would not force or insist on our conversion, and in addition, although we may say we would choose mercy and goodness, in fact we often choose otherwise. It also shows that the Son of God lived as one of us, without sin, and faced the difficulties and activities we experienced, free from evil and hatred – thus providing salvation through Him.

The Gospel states unambiguously all who repent and turn to Christ will be saved. St. Gregory of Nissa discusses the victory of good over evil and shows the wicket will be purged of their evil. My reading is that when the wicked realize God's unconditional love, they would undergo a painful period (a healing period, as if purged of evil by fire) of repentance. In this way, God's unconditional love and perfect justice are experienced by all, as stated by Gregory of Nissa, On the Making of Man:

> . . . it is meet that they should all rejoice in the LORD when they all look towards the Beautiful and the Good, and do everything for the glory of God, no longer instruments of sin. I mean good and evil, must any way attach to us, it is clear that to say a man is not included in the good is a necessary demonstration that he is included in the evil. But then, in connection with evil, we find no honor, no glory, no incorruption, no power.[10]

We express regret when considering such things as cruelty through our intentions and acts. When these are within the context, or criticisms, of God, we pass responsibility for our acts and attributes to something or someone else; yet we entertain the notion that we have the right to choose any act we wish. We usually assess the outcomes of our autonomous choices by the pain or pleasure we experience. The pleasure experienced by us may satisfy us, and consequently we do not see a need to change. The pain of existence may cause us to ignore the choices we have made, and instead appeal to God in some way, or to blame gods for such outcomes. We may attempt to deal with this dichotomy by seeking ways to make our intentions, actions, and morality (goodness)

10. Gregory of Nyssa, *Dogmatic Treatises*, 665.

comprehensible within our community, and articulate desirable (freely chosen) choices by all in that community. The result would be a commonality amongst individuals of the community, in intent, act, so that all outcomes would be common to every member of such a community. This ideal democracy may include an appeal to God to strengthen the community and is testimony to the spirit of humanity, in that it aspires to such an ideal, albeit vaguely understood and poorly practiced. The freedom of the human spirit (discussed previously) provides the ground for a common good, while the experience and history of humanity argue against the ability for human beings to achieve the ideal of the common good.

The death and resurrection of Christ encapsulate the mystery of the faith, as it nullifies the power of sin that results from the law. Anyone who is without sin cannot incur death. Consequently, the death of Christ is contrary to the law, and God resurrects Him into eternal life. Christ has conquered death and provides the way to salvation for all who repent of sin and have faith.

The essential elements of Christianity briefly discussed here, are intended to emphasize the need for our salvation; Christ is the resurrection and the life, and no-one could come to the Father accept through the Son. Christians are totally dependent on Christ for forgiveness and cleansing of their sins. This dependence shows the relationship between those called by God to faith in Christ and this is shown by the practices adopted by the Church. This relationship calls for the one-ness within Christian life, Christian thought, and Christian belief in the One-True-God.

The life of Christ discussed in the Gospels includes healing those who sought Him through faith; Christ taught His disciples, fed the hungry, healed the sick, forgave sins, and engaged with the religious leaders to show them where they had erred. These accounts testify to the mercy and love from Christ to all, including sinners and non-Jews, and illustrates the various responses from people. Christ emphasized the importance of faith while showing to His disciples that the Holy Spirit conferred understanding.

We may undertake a dialogue concerning life, faith, and the love of God, based on the revelation within freedom. Such a dialogue and prayer are possible because the meaning of God's name is within that revelation and this life is sustained through faith in Christ. Faith becomes God-substantiating within the goodness and reason in our daily life. Faith in Christ as the redeemer results from the Holy Spirit, poured into the hearts and souls of those called by God. The reason for this is God's love for humanity, and this has been shown by the fact that God so loved humanity that He gave his only begotten son, so that those who have faith in him would have everlasting life.

Faith also provides the impetus for action in life. It is not a passive state constructed intellectually. Hope is part of faith since hope is required prior to action. Pre-determined outcomes are not required, as this would render hope unnecessary. Faith in Christ as a solid foundation provides the essential ingredient to ensure that action is not considered, or thought, to be futile. Revelation is "out-of-the-world," so faith, hope, and God's love, are from God (not from the world). These are shown in the Bible to be the fruits of the Holy Spirit, as are all Godly attributes, which now become part of the attributes of those saved through faith in Jesus Christ by the grace of God.

The Gospel proclaims that God will offer salvation to all, culminating in a new heaven and a new earth, and all will receive God's boundless grace and love. This proclamation is primarily celebrated during Church liturgy, and the Faith is also referred to as the Way of Life, expressed by Christians collectively and individually. The Introduction in this Volume deals with ideas, beliefs, and touches on theological reflections; the remainder is poetry. The poet uses language to evoke emotion, imagery, and convey complex ideas expressed in a unique manner using different styles and forms. Poetry is a popular medium for religious expression because it allows the poet to express his thoughts and emotions in a creative and artistic way. Poetry is often used to explore religious themes, such as faith, spirituality, and the power of prayer (other forms of art, such as music, painting, and sculpture, can also be used to express religious themes). The choice of medium depends on the author's preference and the message he wants to convey.

Part I

Book One

God of Eternity
LORD of Salvation
Source of all Power
His presence throughout infinity
All Exists by His will
All is known to Him

Amidst glorious splendor
Dazzling perfection
Dwells the LORD of creation.

His voice, crystal peals of thunder,
Resounds throughout His temple.
The dark hidden depths split asunder
At the behest of His will.
Awesome spectacles arise
As His creations come alive.
Billowing clouds are obliterated
By dazzling stabbing rays of light
Emanating from Him
As on the pure flame
He enters His palatial domain.
Like a thousand suns, like molten gold,
Shines His face, eternal God of old.
From His throne's side

A limpid river serenely flows
Into the temple of soft golden light
Lit by seven flames
Whose radiance and luminescence
Is the essence of peace
The river lends its reflection
To this sublime perfection
Harmony and symmetry are its dimensions
    At the center
    Upon an altar
Are written the codes of Eternal life.

        As the Prince of Grace acts
        Creating movement and space;
        Mighty forces arise as he makes His way
        With an extended arm he holds them at bay.
        As the Word utters to create
        All calms to peace
        As if extending an embrace
        To hold him to that place

Heaven; an ocean of Love and Peace.
Angels luxuriate in God's Grace
Gathering to converse with the Light of Heaven
In God's temple, heaven's wondrous crown.

Heaven's host of angels is vast
To whom God gave powers and talents
Setting three above the others
The Archangels:
Gabriel the messenger of his supreme God,
Michael the commander of the host,
Lucifer perfect in art and all knowledge,
Mighty angels serving the Kingdom of the Ages.
The angels increase Heaven's prosperity
Creating great works, marveling at their destiny.
Striving for perfection, angels finding new joys,
The kingdom of heaven prospers in all its ways.

Lucifer contributed great marvels
The center of cultural activities
His intellect illuminating many paths
Angels admire his leadership and talents.
But he began to find greater pleasure,
In the will to power, the desire to rule.
To his closest followers he outlined his scheme.
Heaven was too large and wealthy.
The mighty, he said,
Must rule over the lowly.
He would rule from a throne
An equal to God, to command
Those who swore obedience to him,
Their chosen Sovereign.

He and his allies spread this intrigue,
Seducing angels by his deceit.
Lucifer's confidence grew
As he won a large following.
He dispatched this message to the Most High.

God's reply:

> How art thou fallen from heaven, O day-star, son of the morning! how art thou cut down to the ground, that didst lay low the nations! And thou saidst in thy heart, I will ascend into heaven, I will exalt my throne above the stars of God; and I will sit upon the mount of congregation, in the uttermost parts of the north; I will ascend above the heights of the clouds; I will make myself like the Most High."[1]

Lucifer raged in anger
He commanded his lieutenants to gather
Saying to the angels of his alliance,
"Prepare a crown, a throne, a scepter,
I proclaim myself Sovereign,

1. Isa14:12–14

All this is mine, I reign as god."

He warned his followers their new freedom
Would be taken by the Almighty
Who would send Michael to invade their home
To banish them to eternal doom.

The angels prepared for war
Raphael confirming Lucifer's rebellion
He was declared Satan, the adversary.
God ordered Michael to chain the rebels.

The armies met on a great plane
Each hurling thunderbolts of pain
Engulfing the other in rivers of flame
The ground shook to the armies of angelic force.
Matter disintegrated, planets turned to rubble,
Angels were scattered, maimed, and bruised.
Some losing courage stood in agonized groups.

Michael sliced a wing of Satan's army
Engulfing them in an exploding star
He, a colossus of power
Swept the rebels before him.

Satan tore the center of Michael's army
In a great rage, scattered angels,
Hurling agonizing rays of force.
None could withstand him, until Gabriel
Seeing the havoc of Satan,
Stopped his charge with power
That staggered Satan, and he fell.

The creation groaned under the war
Stars exploded into fearsome nebulae
Heaven shook to its foundations
Fallen angels littered the battlefield in anguish.
    Michael and Gabriel had formed a corps
Battling a group around Satan.

(When Satan fell before Gabriel
his troop rushed to his aid
protecting him as he regained his strength).
Most of his army had fallen,
Proud Satan fought on
Attacked from every side,
They held their ground.

Twice Michael hurled javelins of flame,
Burning into the spirit's innermost being,
Satan fought on and would not yield
Such was Satan's perversity, his fanaticism complete.

Michael cried, "I pray God may bring you down
Rebellious spirit, your war will destroy the creation."

God's voice thundered from above,
"Fallen, fallen, is the author of sin."

Satan staggered, fear in his eyes,
Stumbling as one gone blind
Helpless before the Archangels
Unable to continue the fight.
Michael proclaimed in a loud voice,
"Destroyer, the spirit who despises perfection
Behold the chains of your condemnation,
To hold you in the pits of hell, your kingdom,
There to receive obedience from malicious spirits
Who with you, have lost all beauty and glory.
Receive your just reward, O angel of fury."

The evil spirits were thrown into hell
Like lightning they fell
Into the raging flames of hell.
Cries of hysteria, anguish, and rage,
Filled that dark God-forsaken place.
Once beautiful angels now became
Malformed demons living in torment

Utterly damned.

God removed all that damaged Heaven
Comforting its inhabitants by saying:

> Sons of Heaven created by My hand
> Hear the voice of your God
> Be not troubled by evil
> Nor fear Satan and his demons
> Those who defy the Divine Will
> Are burdened with their own deed
> Having forsaken goodness and life
> Their lot is eternal darkness and strife
> On planet earth I will create humanity
> By Grace and Faith, they shall be sons of the Almighty
> Through deeds of strength, courage, and dedication,
> Shall God's angels rejoice in beautification.

Solemnly singing hymns of praise
Angels worshipped our Eternal God.

Book Two

> The Heavens declare the glory of God; and the firmament shows his handy work. Day unto day utters speech, and night to night shows knowledge.[1]

He brooded over the troubled planet.

Continents cracked
Volcanoes erupted
Molten lava flowed as sulfurous clouds
Saturated the air with acidic fumes.
The violent convulsions
Rent the heart of the planet
Seas flooded land masses
Hurricanes devastating the surface.

He corrected its orbit and tilt,
Giving it summer, autumn, winter, and spring.
The sun shone brilliantly in clear blue skies
Seas gently lapped golden shores
Vegetation covered the land with emerald green
Embroidered with a rainbow of flowers
Magic beams of moonlight lit the night
The day filled with a chorus of sounds
From animals in pasture
Oceans swarmed with a myriad of creatures.

The sapphire planet hung in the velvet night of space
Rejoicing under the care of its Creator.

Angels marveled and sang.
God took a lump of earth,
Shaping into a man
Breathing into him the spirit of life.

In God's image was Adam created
To live on this beautiful planet.

1. Ps 19:1–2

He made a companion for man
To further all life in joy,
He made them male and female
For love, for happiness, forever.

When God completed His work, He rested
Feeling refreshed He blessed that day
The Sabbath rest brings peace to the weary
The faithful receive joy from the LORD.

In the cool of the evening
God instructed Adam and Eve.
"All in this garden is for you,
I made it for your good.
    The fruit of the tree—knowledge of good and evil
You must not eat
That will bring you death.
Live and do not taste its fruit.
You are placed in this paradise
To live with joy in your Creator's grace."

News of this marvel
Spread throughout the creation.
All creatures, in heaven or in a dark place,
Talked of the wonder performed by God.

In the depths of tormenting hell
The news inspired fierce passions among the damned.
In their hatred they swore and cursed God.
Satan ordered the commotion to cease,
"Cease your babbling and unite your wits
Think of a way to destroy what is His."
The demons sank in blank despondency
Their prison was impenetrable
Worse waited them without
Dangers from which they shrank.
To his macabre crowd the proud angel outlined his plan,
"I shall cause these new creatures to stumble

To choose against Him who put us in chains
Making us angels worse than the slain."
He crossed unknown barriers
Sustained forces tearing out his brain
Crossed the terrifying thunderous terrain.
Battered and bruised, the ancient being
Rested a short distance from earth.

With appealing sounds, the snake talked to Eve.
"And what has God told you, beautiful Eve?"
"The fruit of the tree of knowledge—good and evil
God commands we must not eat," said Eve
"But look how good the fruit is," he said,
"You can almost taste its sweet flavor.
"Know from me, innocent Eve
"God forbids that which He wants to keep
"For on the day you eat its fruit
"You will be as gods, above good and evil.

Eve considered the serpent's words
Eyeing the tree and its delicious fruit
As desire began to grow in her heart
This, she realized, was the truth.
She plucked the fruit
Excited, she took a bite;
Then, thinking of Adam, she ran gaily
Saying, "O Adam, I have eaten of the forbidden tree
"Taste it, it is so sweet,
We will be like gods, above good and evil."

Adam felt a sudden fear, saying, "What is this?"
Eve chattered, and he wondered if it mattered
What did God mean we will die?
Eve has already eaten it and she lived.

While she waited in anticipation
A feeling of power grew with the conception
That he was independent.

Taking the fruit, he ate it for her to see.
"There," he said, and bravely threw the core away.

Adam looked at Eve, naked and soft
His desire for her increased.
He felt he was her master.
Eve admired his strength and independence.
Suddenly she blushed, in her shame
And innocence, she began to cry.

At this Adam floundered, forgetting his pride
Strangely he said, "We are naked, we must hide
God may see us like this, hurry."

God came for his conversation with them
Adam and Eve were not there to greet Him.
He called, and Adam answered from a grove,
"We are not dressed, we cannot come."

"Who has told you this?" cried God
"Have you eaten of the forbidden tree?"
Adam felt afraid at the sound of God's voice.
"It was Eve," he said, "She gave me the fruit."
"It was the snake," said Eve, "He told me to eat."

Once sin enters your earth, it will suffer
Eve, when you become a mother
You will know pain and sorrow.
Adam, sweat will cover your brow
By hard work you will earn your bread.
You have not obeyed the will of your God
The earth will grow thorns and weeds
Mankind will weep because of his sins.

Gabriel and Michael, with another ten
Accosted the devil on his way back to hell.

He laughed when he saw them
Asking how matters were on the earth

He had heard of their celebration and song
Why did they have such angry looks?
Has something gone amiss?
Michael spoke, "Source of all evil
Well-named you are the devil
Do you believe you can strive with He who is life?"
"Then why this merry company?"
Was the devil's reply
"Will you visit me thus often? Tell me
So I may prepare some fruit for you to eat."
As the devil laughed Gabriel interrupted,
"The LORD God punishes you for this evil,
Your torment, like your work, has only begun
Horrors&destruction&sins will originate from you."

With malice in his eyes, Satan
Entered hell and declared a celebration.
Demons danced amongst the shadows of hell
Others retold the story of how Adam fell.
At the height of these festivities, a silence descended
Demons dreadful fears apprehended
Seeing each other as monsters, horribly deformed,
Satan was transformed into a huge snake.
They cried out, some hiding from the sight
Hell filled with loud rumbling thunder
Every place cracked asunder
Ruins were added to ruins
As Satan began to shriek as one gone mad.

Book Three

> For I know that nothing good dwells within me, that is, in my flesh. I can will what is right, but I cannot do it. For I do not do the good I want, but the evil I do not want is what I do. Now if I do what I do not want, it is no longer I that do it, but sin which dwells within me.[1]

Once man disobeys the Divine Will
He is impure, therein dwells sin,
No longer to commune with God
Mankind stands alone.
He who felt that the choice was his
Now looks with longing at the gifts
Wonders how it was all lost;
Perhaps offence comes before repentance.

Adam felt sorrow, Eve no less.
But it was being deprived of luxury and ease
That sorrowed the parents of mankind.
God covered their shame
Did not bring them hurt nor blame
But warned them of life's mishaps.
Lest they should now seek eternal life
Angels with swords of fire
Guarded the entrance from where they came.

Adam and Eve entered a land grown wild
Working for their food
Waiting and hoping each day anew.

Human history dawned when Adam and Eve sinned
Mankind continued adding sin to sin.

Cain killed Able
From envy and spite.
Man's punishment

1. Rom 7:18–20

He could not bear it.
He prayed for God's mercy.
The earth would not sustain him
For he polluted the earth with his deed
All men would wish to kill him
Becoming a wonderer amongst mankind.

They took any women they desired
Becoming sexually depraved
God's Spirit saw vice and brutality,
Brother treated brother with cruelty
Corruption increased with every newborn
Until Satan considered earth his new home.
God was sorry he had made mankind

The Eternal One sent a flood
To destroy mankind
He saved the good man Noah.
Yet each generation continued in evil
The ways of mankind were the ways of the devil.

God called Abram to leave the city of sin
Where humans were sacrificed,
Women prostituted in temples to worship idols

Abram left all to commune with God
Wondering through the land seeking God
Finding faith from God
Becoming the friend of God.

He took Isaac, the son promised by God
In obedience to sacrifice him to God.
The Angel of the LORD said to Abraham
"Your faith in God is complete,
God does not desire sacrifice of sons
But obedience and faith."

God kept his promise to his friend Abraham
To his descendants, the children of Israel.

Part I

God delivered Israel from Egypt
Giving the law through Moses
Israel was sanctified and given the covenant
A generation guided by Moses in the wilderness
Until their children inherited the promised land.
God sent his prophets to Israel
To guide them into God's way of life
Israel was blessed in every way

But Israel turned away from Jehovah
Disobeying his law and his prophets
Choosing to worship idols made by man's hand.
Suffering grew as Israel turned to heathen ways.

The flesh with its corruption
Brought ruin to the creation
Mankind raped virgin valleys
Turned gardens into deserts.

Armies fought and destroyed
Greedy men laid waste what remained.
The race of corruption stilled the sounds of birds
Destroyed the flowers of the field.
Every intent of man's heart was evil continuously
Surely Satan had won a great victory
Proclaimed false prophets and priests
As dark religions grew, adding to man's misery.
These sons of darkness sought Satanic mysteries
Knowledge to add to the load of slaves
Serving monsters united to the spirit of perdition.

Just men were often hunted
Merciless men shut them in prison
Killing and maiming God's prophets.
In a world sorely distressed
Few could find God, or be blessed
By the comfort that comes from Him whose behest
Our forefathers disobeyed, thus opening the road

To all our woes, life's many pains and loads.

Elijah was a prophet of God
With power greater than the sword
He brought to shame the prophets of Baal
Most of whom he slew.
Jezebel the harlot made him afraid
He fled into the desert, wishing that he died.
The prophet full of the Spirit of Might
Felt helpless before the forces of night,
Righteous men lose hope and take to flight
Elijah became disheartened
Believing there was no faith in Israel.
Yet, God was content with seven thousand
From the multitude of Israel.
Elijah faced his troubles
Serving God and his nation.
On a chariot of fire, he went to his peace
Full of God's Spirit and grace.

Isaiah was a prophet some proclaimed mad
Who raged about hell and the damned
A hard man, who would chastise
Hated by those filled with Satan's malice.
The prophet who proclaimed justice for the nations
The end of our sufferings through God's progress
Was condemned by brutish men
Who delude the nation.

In their hypocrisy men proclaim liberal ways
God, they stated, demanded harsh trials
Was unforgiving and His servants fools
Liberty would come from their minds
But alas to those who chose to think otherwise;
Prison, torture, social injustice,
Is the liberty brought by men of oppression.

Man wanted to choose, and by choice

Chose sin and a life of lies,
With sophistication, eloquence, great lengthy verse
Covered the original, making it more perverse.

Though choosing to search for the truth
Mankind found it easier to delude
Listening to comfortable lies
They laughed at any who chose otherwise
Demanding choice for himself
He deprived another that choice.

Neither sin to God nor to man deterred progress
Systems of organization and social order grew
Barbarity was hidden and culture flowered.
They sought to behave, show manners and poise
Despising the crude barbaric hordes.
The classes of power and privilege grew
Filled palaces with classical beauty found anew.
The church, the state, institutions of law and order
Men of genius built for their glory and power.

Intelligent men sought knowledge
To free mankind from superstition
The burden of mysterious dark religion.
The wise pondered;
Could knowledge free mankind so plundered
Over centuries by misery and evil.
History shows with every new idea
Trials and hardships grew and began anew.

They left farms for factories of darkness
To work endless hours for a crust of bread
Children laboring in coal mines
Women working as beasts of burden
For the birth of the industrial revolution.
France threw of the yoke of tyranny
Slaughtering the aristocracy and monarchy
Replacing them with sadistic monsters

Who founded the politics of the hordes.

Neighbor spied on neighbor
Anyone with an opinion was a traitor
Blood flowed freer then free speech
Cruelty, anarchy and the hag's screech
Proclaimed freedom, liberty and fraternity
To bring in the birth of democracy.

From the dark ages of superstition and ignorance
Man progressed to the days of enlightenment
To science, religious freedom, the creative arts
Until he began to believe he could live and be free.

But he lived to slaughter by the millions
Using guns, bombs, and poisonous gases
As mankind used the gifts of the sciences.

During the days of peace
Industry and commerce increase
Mankind uses his talents to create a metropolis
Destroying the beauty nature gives us freely.

He does this, he says, to bring prosperity
Each family can grow with health and vitality.
Yet he pollutes the air we breathe
Destroys the family, alienates children, and oppresses women.

Crime rises like a great serpent's head,
People live in ugly monstrosities all their days;
Diseases are cured, as people eat food without nourishment
Suffering anxiety, neurosis, and insecurity.

Mankind continued in the ways of sin
Finding only the things that it can bring
Sin corrupts and this corruption spreads
Deluding man's heart, destroying his sense.

The spirit of mankind is un-nourished, imprisoned.
Alienated from God

Man could not find that so freely offered
The love and care of his Creator
Whose will is for mankind to live and be free.

The prophets spoke the word of God
Proclaiming the coming of the Son of God
Who would save us from Satan's way to death
Into the resurrection and the Way of Life.

Part II

Book One

God's Mercy
is infinite
God's Grace
is boundless
God's Will
is for humanity
to live according to His divine Love.

God has shed his Love
in our hearts.
God has given His Son
to be our Redeemer.
God has poured his Holy Spirit
for our salvation.

The birth of Christ:

Born of the Holy Spirit
His mother a Holy Virgin
Giving birth to God as Man
Descended from Abraham and David.

Shepherds came to a manger
Wise men followed a bright star
To bring gifts to the new-born king
All worshipped the Son of God

Angels joyously sang of Salvation.

He grew in grace and knowledge
Debating the law with the elders
Performing his Father's work
In God's Holy Temple.

The Spirit of God descending like a dove
And a voice from heaven above,
"This is my son, the beloved,
With whom I am well pleased."[1]

Jesus began to preach:
"Repent, the kingdom of heaven is amongst you.
Peter, Andrew, James, John, I have called you
With your brothers and sisters to follow me."
He taught the people
Who were astonished at his authority
The Word of God.
All could see and hear
People flocked to the son of man
Who healed the sick and cured the lame.

Jesus, hear
our great sorrows;
Christ, heal
our many afflictions;
Jesus, forgive
our sins.

Christ the Redeemer
Our High Priest
Went to the mount, saying:
Blessed are those
    Who are poor in spirit
Blessed are those

1. Matt 3:1–3: And Jesus increased in wisdom and stature and in favor with God and man. In those days came John the Baptist, preaching in the wilderness of Judea, "Repent, for the kingdom of heaven is at hand."

Who hunger for what is right
Blessed are those
Who are merciful
Blessed are those
Who are of a pure heart
Blessed are those
Who seek to bring peace
Blessed are you who hear his words
You shall be the sons and daughters of God.

I have come to fulfil the law and the prophets.

This is the law of God.
Do not have hatred in your heart
Forgive your brothers and sisters
Then come to the altar of God.
This is the law of Jesus.
Do not look with lust at a woman,
If your eye causes you to sin
Pluck it out and throw it away.
This is the law from God.
If anyone strikes you, turn the other cheek
Love your enemies
Do good to those who despise you.
This is the law from Christ
Our Father causes the sun to rise
For the evil and the good
Be perfect like your Father in heaven.
This is the gift of Jesus Christ
Be not anxious about your life
Seek first the kingdom of heaven,
And all of life's goodness will be yours.

His disciples asked him, *"Show us God."*
You have seen me
You have seen God
If you have a small amount of faith
You will say to a mountain of troubles

Be drowned in the deep blue sea
And it will be so.
The faith in Christ
We are born of water and Spirit
God so loved the world that he gave his only son
So that we may have eternal life
He who honors the son
Honors the Father.
He who believes in the Son
Believes in the Father.
He who found life in the son
Will find eternal life in the Father.

A gentile heard the words of Christ
His heart was filled with joy
He said, "Good teacher, your words are pure
like the dew from Heaven."
Yet his heart was troubled
His thoughts in turmoil.
"How could any man be perfect,
To become a son of God?"

God look down on this sinner
Grant me your forgiveness
Show me your mercy
Reveal to me the footsteps
Of your only begotten son.

The law of God is just
It is purity to my soul
He shows me the path of peace
Love is his holy word.

If my eye offends me, oh LORD
If my heart and mind contain impurity
The blood of your son will clean me
I will find joy in your Word.
As I die to sin

I will find salvation
By rebirth in water and the Spirit
I will find salvation
By faith in the son of God
Who has reconciled us to my Father
I will find the bread of life.

Jesus Christ, the revelation of God,
Came to us as the Word of God.
God has granted all authority to the son.
No-one can come to the son,
Unless it is willed by the Father;
His will is the will of the Father.
No-one comes to God
Until cleaned by the blood of the lamb of God.

I came before the throne of God
Asking how I can follow his son.
Although I asked, no answer could I hear,
Until I understood that I am a sinner.

I went into God's Temple
To hear the word of God,
I listened without comprehension,
Not understanding that I am a sinner.

I contemplated the priests' liturgy.
Incense poured on the congregation
I felt aware of something Holy.
Do I understand that I am a sinner?

My heart became troubled.
Since my childhood
I have harmed no man
Nor broken a sacred covenant.

What is my sin?
Can I take the awful burden
This stain of guilt?

What is my crime?

I considered:
Can I approach the Sacred?
Can man contend with God?
Who can utter
Holy, holy, holy, the LORD God?[2]

I heard the LORD's prayer as a child.
The speech to our heavenly Father
Was in my mother's tongue.
Now I stand with questions
About guilt and evil and good and justice
While the world around me is filled with tears
And my life is filled with joys and sorrows

I came before the word of God,
To ask, can I hear the words of the son?

Let us pray for repentance.

2. Rev 4: 9–11. Day and night without ceasing they sing, "Holy, holy, holy, the LORD God the Almighty, who was and is and is to come. "And whenever the living creatures give glory and honor and thanks . . . the twenty-four elders fall before the one who is seated on the throne and worship the one who lives forever and ever . . . "

Book Two

The son said to the Father,
"They are without hope
their ways are to death
their mind is always far from you.
I will save them from the ways of sin
I will offer myself in their place
as a sacrifice, perfect in your sight
for the forgiveness of their sins."

The fear of the LORD is the beginning of knowledge; fools despise wisdom and instruction.

The Elder spoke before the Children:

> Hear, my child, your father's instruction, and do not reject your mother's teaching; for they are a fair garland for your head, and pendants for your neck.[1]

The rebellious angel defied God
So awful his deed; to contradict God
Angel becoming a contradiction,
Heaven's affliction: there is no comprehension

Of the angel perfect in knowledge and art
Impossibly performing in deed and intent
Synthesis of his-self in self-willing
How can man or angel understand this?
Can a created being stand against God?

Of this the wise ponder
The righteous consider,
Who can rationalize the creation of sin?
So dreadful, this deed of Satan
Amazing the angelic host in its secrecy,
Leaving mankind with unparalleled mystery.
How can a being defy his creator God?

1. Prov 1:8–18

Yet deed is preceded by intent,
From whence then arises intent?
Lucifer by art and knowledge,
Did imbued activity with meaning.
Can mankind understand this?

To synthesize is to create from what-is.
How does a self-re-create after God created the self?
(only God creates from nothing)
Did Satan from his-self make, other-than-self?
Lucifer, initially as God's creation
Acted in accordance with God's will,
Now, in the evil deed, he was rend
Into a dilemma, a contradiction.
Satan as his own affliction,
From his intent and act sprang self-will,
Separated from the freedom of God's will.
In this self-will imprisoned
To become punishment of the damned.

Caught in his eternal contradiction
The cause of his own damnation
Satan rages against freedom
While waging war against the Kingdom.
An adversary of heaven's sublime perfection
Known by his ugly action
Satan irrationally destroys the creation.
As a creature of ugly intent, he does imagine
By choosing beasts that were once men
He will afflict those God created
As he had afflicted
Those in heaven whom he beguiled.

He, with a snake's hiss
Tempted those who in heavenly bliss
Communed with their creator God.
Satan deceiving Eve, the mother of humanity.
By this deed he hoped to destroy our eternity

Life granted to all who sprang from her womb.

Satan causing Adam to feel forlorn
Taking his beautiful Eve
Into the dreaded home of Satanic gloom.
It is these deeds that re-created him
Into the adversary, by his own intention.

From within himself Lucifer did provide
His other-than-self. "A god," he said, "am I
To rule the Angelic host from on high."
A contradiction can but destroy.
The soul that synthesizes so from self-life
Destroys life-self, while trying to make sense
Of deed and intent bereft of all reason and rhyme.

Subsequently, such an altered life-self-awareness
Annihilates, while perverted reason synthesizes
Another that cannot be named, senseless
Reason in ruin, without an identity,
Names another as the source of eternity.
This ruin is the death of the soul.

Who shall free mankind from this living death?
Perverse reason, contradicting mankind's self-identity.

Who shall show that God's goodness is the bread of life?
Freeing mankind from eternal strife.

The Elder spoke before the Children:

> Now may the God of peace, who brought back from the dead our LORD Jesus, the great shepherd of the sheep, by the blood of the eternal covenant, make you complete in everything good so that you may do his will, working among us that which is pleasing in his sight, through Jesus Christ, to whom be the glory forever and ever Amen.[2]

2. Heb 13:20–21

> Wisdom cries out in the street; in the squares she raises her voice. . ."How long, O simple ones, will you love being simple? How long will scoffers delight in their scoffing and fools hate knowledge? Give heed to my reproof; I will pour out my thoughts to you; I will make my words known to you.[3]

(A simple one replied)
"God has made
God can unmake
He is God of all he has created.
How can we be blamed
These matters are beyond our comprehension!

God is compassionate,
He will not rage or in anger blame
He knows our weakness, why we sin.
No perfection do we in self-righteousness claim.
We beg God to remove our shame
Satan created sin and he should receive the blame."

The Elder spoke before the Children:

> My child, if you accept my words and treasure up my commandments within you, making your ear attentive to wisdom and inclining your heart to understanding; . . . then you will understand the fear of the LORD and find the knowledge of God.[4]

"But surely," said the simple one,
"God has chosen his holy one
Pouring His Spirit on him, granting grace.
Though sin brings death as it's wage
His commandments guide our ways
He instructs us by His Prophets"

The Elder continued:

3. Prov 1:20–23
4. Prov 2:1–19.

> For the LORD gives wisdom; from his mouth comes knowledge and understanding; . . . Then you will understand righteousness and justice and equity, every good path; for wisdom will come into your heart, and knowledge will be pleasant to your soul.

"I will put my faith in the LORD"
Said the simple one, "I will believe
Without anxiety or fear, I will live
By following instructions from God's servant
Whom God has called to serve His people
Within Mother Church will I be nourished
Protected from the evil one who destroys."

The Elder (with a sigh) continued:

> It will save you from the way of evil, from those who speak perversely, . . . who rejoice in doing evil and delight in the perverseness of evil; . . . and who are devious in their ways.

Once sin enters our heart
We can no longer be of clear intent
With reason we struggle to understand
Our own deeds intended as virtuous
Benign to our fellowman
Yet these same deeds
Before our eyes are evil in outcome.
The good we comprehend
In deed, becomes the opposite effect.

Our spirit
Struggles with this perplexing cause and effect
We have, through sacrifice and good intent
Brought comfort to those suffering from such effects.
Yet, though we seem
Trapped in perplexity and fear
The human spirit continues to soar
Attempting to get nearer

To the source of all goodness and truth.

> You will be saved from the loose woman, from the adulteress with her smooth words, who . . . forgets her sacred covenant; for her way leads down to death, and her paths to the shades; . . .

Go to the LORD with a grateful heart
Bring an offering of gratitude to Him
Do not bow to greedy men
Your welfare is God's interest
Of sin do not inquire
The evil woman do not desire
(For who knows his own heart?)
God is the source of wisdom
He provides for our reason.
Offer a pleasing sacrifice to God
Forsake the ways of evil
Go to God's sacred temple
Wherein the Holy Spirit dwells
Plead with Him for guidance
Remember God's forbearance
The human race exists by God's grace
Let God set your spirit free
Come before the LORD with a grateful heart
In the silent beauty meditate on His word.

> Then all the congregation . . . came, everyone whose heart was stirred, and everyone whose spirit was willing, and brought the LORD's offering to be used for the tent of meeting, and for all its service, and for the sacred vestments . . . all sorts of gold objects, everyone bringing an offering of gold to the LORD . . . , so that all the artisans . . . said to Moses, "The people are bringing much more than enough for doing the work . . ." So the people were restrained from bringing;[5]

5. Exod 35:20—36:8

Come before the Temple of God
Worship in Holiness the Sacred Word
Cleanse yourself from evil
Forsake the ways of the world
Enter the Temple of God
Within your heart inscribe the law
Meditate on His commandments
May God illuminate your understanding.

The Son of Man

Born in Perfection

Conceived by the Holy Spirit
Born from the virgin Mary.
Jesus, free from sin that afflicts mankind;
In this perfection God became man.

Born the Savior

Jesus Christ, from the blessed virgin
The handmaiden of God, in the flesh
Jesus Christ was thus born
To save those conceived in sin.

Born for the Sacred Covenant

To suffer the effects of the flesh.
Though Satan tempted the Son of God
("If you are the Son of God,
Turn these stones into bread.")
This Word of God in the flesh,
Lived according to the word of God.

Born to serve

To be the greatest servant of all
The Son of God, sent to save sinners.
This son of man born of Mary
Came to save those born of the promise.
The captain of our Salvation,
In whose footpaths those called by God
Tread as works of Faith.
Our Savior before God, so we may
Conform according to his life.

Born the Son of God
To bring before God his brothers and sisters.
(Who are my brothers, who is my mother?
Who are my sisters?
You whom the Father has called).
Christ
Jesus, the Word of God
Did to our lowly estate stoop
Did not aspire to great height
But came close to our sufferings
Jesus
By his life did bring
God's Comforter
Our desire now to be
Obedient to God's Holy Will
Christ
As a sacrifice from God
To be sacrificed for us before God;
This sacrifice was not of human invention
Nor against Satan a heroic intention

(Such things are not of the Sacred Will
God does not recognize
Any not derived from His Holiness.
. . . To those verses on Satan and his fall
I say forget them all [6]
Be guided by the Will of God)
Jesus
His purpose, the Word of God
Intent and act, reason and heart, all One;
The living Son of God for our sake did come
To walk in this world of sorrows
To hear and see our human woes
To heal us from our own effects

6. Matt 4:10–11 Jesus said to him, away with you, Satan! for it is written, "Worship the LORD your God, and serve only him." Then the devil left him, and suddenly angels came and waited on him.

To bring before God
Sons and daughters as Heaven's citizens.
Christ
The High priest of the Holy Temple
Though for himself need not atone
Made himself the atonement for us all.
Jesus
The Son of God who at God's right hand did sit
Now stood before the judgement seat
Not for his own sins to hear judgement
Rather for our hopeless ways to find salvation
To dissolve the effects of sin
That we took from he who
Polluted our souls and destroyed our reason.
Christ
Came for the cleansing
That we may follow in His footsteps
That our prayers God will hear.
This is rebirth of water and the Spirit
Jesus
The Faith from God
By resurrection into the Savior of life;
It is for this that Jesus Christ was born.

As the Word of God created life
So the Living Word of God came to bring life
His dying denied the effects of sin
Bringing us that which we to ourselves deny
Life free from contradictions
Reason dedicated to the good life.
Christ on this earth came
Living as the living proof of God's intent
To make life everlasting our destiny.

From the first Adam we progress
Unto Christ the final creation
Heaven's personified bliss

Perfect in grace and obedient to the divine will;
Christ first lived amongst us to show the divine gift
Life from God; this is the Kingdom of God,
No burden, no slavery, no misery, no vice,
Christ showed by his deeds and God's grace
The life that God gladly grants to His own;
    The life in Christ perfects the human soul.

    God has willed it before the beginning
All to share in the love of God
God gave his law to Moses
His promise to Abraham.
    The prophets spoke to the children of Israel
The holy ones saw in vision the Almighty
Who kept faith with Abraham
Kept the holy seed for His purpose
    God hardened the hearts of sinners
Showing His patience to His chosen ones
Israel was given Moses; but those above twenty perished
Wandering in the desert with the truth before them
(Except Joshua and Caleb who desired the land promised by God).
    God send his Son to the people of Judea
They rejected the Word of God,
God's power was manifest to all
Yet they chose to reject the Light of Life
    God so determined; those in darkness to see the light
    Salvation to be known throughout the earth.

As the manna rained from heaven
Unto the children of Israel
So God's goodness pours forth
Unto each portion of the earth
Food from God to sustain the weary
Hope for the goodness we so passionately desire
Faith in Christ to fill us with life each day
A shield from the evil we fear.

LORD God of all, this Godly fear
Is not a source of wisdom to the world.
It is we in Christ that comprehend
The suffering that evil pours on the human race
Even as they deny God's Son
Some scorning the message from on High.

This day I set before you life and blessings[7]
Faith in the Son of Man who is the way of life.
Choose life; forsake all evil and bless those weary
Of the ways of sin, even as they walk death's way.

The Servant[8]
Everywhere he went, people came to see this man.
Who was he? How will history judge him?
He preached to those with whom he grew up as a child
They listened with disbelief and wanted to throw him off a cliff.
He healed the man who could not enter the pool
When it was stirred by the Angel of Israel
Sternly saying, "Do not tell them who has healed you
Glorify God lest worst befalls you."
(This man of Israel refused to heed and told the Pharisees).
He talked to the Samaritan woman of her wayward ways
The city believed because of her
But then believed because of Jesus the Christ
Many glorified God because of Christ.
He cleared the peddlers out of the temple
Insisting people pray to God, not to a market place

7. Deut 30:19–20 "I call heaven and earth to witness against you today that I have set before you life and death, blessings and curses. Choose life so that you and your descendants may live, loving the LORD your God."

John 10:10 "I came that they may have life, and have it abundantly."

1 Pet 3:9–13 "Do not repay evil for evil or abuse for abuse; but, on the contrary, repay with a blessing, that you might inherit a blessing."

8. Isa 52:13. "Behold, My Servant shall deal prudently; He shall be exalted and extolled and be very high."

Matt 8:16–17 ". . . and cured all who were sick. This was to fulfil what had been spoken through the prophet Isaiah, 'He took our infirmities and bore our diseases.'"

(Showing that we are the Temple of the Holy Spirit).
The Pharisees and other hypocrites demanded a sign,
"Show us your authority," they cried in disdain.
The Holy Temple shall be brought down
And God will raise it up in three days
To the glory of God and the salvation of mankind.

Unto whom was Christ sent?
And to whom did he bring comfort?
To the common people,
Those who sought God's way of life.

Who followed Jesus where-ever he went?
And who listened to his words with wonderment?
Those who showed pity to the poor
And those who worshiped God of Israel.

Unto whom did the Word appear?
And who saw the splendid vision
Of Moses and the Prophets?
Fishermen from Galilee, men like you and me.

Throughout the land the Son of Man spoke
People crowding about him, the sick and the lame,
"Oh, but to touch his garment and be cured."
The power moved from him, so he looked around,
    "Your faith has healed you," he said to her.

    "Go to the people, be compassionate,"
He said to his disciples,
"See how plentiful the harvest is!
Plant the seed; bring the Word amongst
The people with faith in their hearts
They are our brothers and sisters."

To this day faith for life
Is found in people's hearts
They feel the weariness of the world
They struggle with contradictions

Taught in schools and churches
Knowledge of this world, such foolishness, without faith
They prattle on, those wise in their own sight.

Walk with me upon that path
Where our Savior bore his cross
The women crying at the sight
An innocent man beaten and bruised
Unable to walk with the heavy wood
Unto which he would be nailed

Hear his words with me,
"Do not cry for me. Cry for yourselves, for what awaits you."
Thousands died as the fanatical Jews
Once again forgot their prophets and laws
Following death's way and against Rome,
(and more amongst themselves)
Fought for nought but grotesque distortions
Of the sublime message of Moses and the Prophets.
They forsook the faith of their father Abraham
These descendants of Abraham, born of the promise
Followed hypocritical leaders, who in degenerate ways
Distorted the word, and made others
More the children of hell than themselves.

> All we like sheep have gone astray; we have all turned to our own way, and the LORD has laid on him the iniquity of us all.[9]

Look with me down history's road
The footsteps mankind has trod
After the Word, the Apostles, the Saints,
After the Martyrs' hymns had reached Him on High,
See the great institutions built in Christ's name
Examine history's account of Pope and Patriarch
Who with greater bitterness than Pharisee and Sadducee
Worse than the Jew they despised, in hypocritical ways

9. Isa 53:6

Distorted and abused the Holy Word of God
While millions sought the meaning of the gospel
In Church liturgy and priestly service
Each Sabbath people obey the edicts
Decreed by priest and church.

Look down history's road and look at today
For these same hypocrisies blemish each day,
The people to this day follow the Son of Man
The ground is as fertile as when he walked in Galilee.
But what of the efforts of the clergy
Or the prophets of materialism's false faith?
Who to this day spread their deceit
After Jesus Christ, the revelation of God
Was crucified on the cross!

> He was oppressed, and he was afflicted, yet he did not open his mouth; . . . By a perversion of justice, he was taken away . . . although he had done no violence, and there was no deceit in his mouth.[10]

This day they preach social justice
Last time I listened, they blest soldiers
Who marched into battle.
Today one considered wise speaks of truth and science
Knowing as he speaks, that science
Shows he is a liar and a fool.
This day they talk of pity for the poor and dispossessed
The politicians who yesterday
Corrupted the nation to feed the rich.

I heard of a man wounded in battle
A warrior, a killer of men, who excelled in destruction,
Repented to become a man of God.
Dedicating himself to good works
In the face of greater terror than the gun
Embracing poverty and lack of worldly pride.

10. Isa 53:7

I know that today, as in yester-year
Men and women in saintly ways abide,
To the poor and oppressed they bring hope
Some may be clergy, some of worldly ways
Who bring light in the darkness,
To guide people through anguish and distress.

Just as people flocked to hear
Christ speak on the hill of Judea
So today people desire the message.
They long to hear of hope,
For the happiness that alludes so many.

> Out of the anguish of his soul he shall see and be satisfied; by his knowledge shall the righteous one, my servant, make many to be accounted righteous, and he shall bear their iniquities . . .because he hath poured out his soul unto death: and he was numbered with the transgressors; and he bare the sin of many, and made intercession for the transgressors.[11]

Faith and truth abide in people's hearts
In spite of the universal grave that never says enough.
Hope, faith, the freedom from God on high
Has never left this earth and is found night and day.
Desire for freedom in the human spirit, like a flame
Burns, in spite of the deceit dampening that flame;
It can never be extinguished, for the Son of Man
Did unto the Cross walk, to suffer for man.
Faith, hope, charity; these are fruits of the Comforter
Given to God's saints because of the Savior.

Why did the Son of God die?
Why did the son of man walk amongst us that day?
Why does God look unto a world in distress
He who would gladly bless us all in one moment?

How does the Holy Spirit of God abide in the Saints,

11. Isa 53:11–12

As they bear the anguish of those in sorry plight?
How would God forgive the sins of you and me?
He, the sacred being on high.

These things God has revealed to us through the Spirit;[12]

In a vision my spirit beheld
A wondrous sight—the Son of Man

I beheld a world in peace
In which all the people rejoiced
On their faces a light shone
The Spirit filled them with love divine
Every gesture and thought a prayer
Of gratitude and thanks
    An offering for the Prince of Peace.

My spirit beheld over centuries of time
Mankind progressing against the oppressor, whom we despise
For the suffering and affliction that fills the earth.
Though humanity to the brink of destruction would come,
We turned away because of the sacrifice of the Son.
God in His Mercy decreed
Mankind lives according to His divine Will.

I asked the elder to explain to me
When will my splendid vision come to pass
I wished to rejoice for humanity
To sing and tell my neighbor,
"Oh, come and believe
Suffering will end, our tears will cease
No more oppressors, no more deceit
We shall live in joy and be free."
My vision filled me with wonder
So I asked the elder
When will mankind live in such splendor?

The elder replied with a look of sorrow.

12. 1Cor 2:9–16

"Look to the covenant,
The law, the signs from above
The manna from heaven,
The rock that gave water to the dessert.
None over the age of twenty entered the promised land
Wandering in the desert for forty years.
For forty days they spied on the promised land
But only Joshua and Caleb believed
Putting their trust in the LORD.

Moses' faith was tested at the rock, in his anger,
Sorely vexed by the children of Israel.
The LORD saying, "See the promised land from afar."
Moses died on the Mount. The stubborn people of Israel
In the desert wondered, eating the bread from heaven.
Until a generation free from the ways of Egypt
Entered the promised land."

I argued, saying to the elder,
"God has given the holy seed
To be the source of virtue and reason
The saints of the Most High walk amongst the oppressed
As witnesses to the mercy of God and His Holy Intent."

The elder replied,
"The Son of God was crucified
By men and women who despise the law
They and you walk the ways of sin
Evil intent and deceit are hidden within.
When you appear to choose the good
Before God you choose evil
Believing this is good;
Sin has corrupted your soul. Your acts
Which you hope will bring goodness
Instead, within your life (hidden from you)
Bring the evil.

The Son of God obeyed unto death

To Godly intent He died.
This sacrifice Christ made
According to Divine Will.
Mankind to this day portrays
The death of the Son of God as an act
Within the rituals of a community.

Preach for man to repent!
Urge mankind to turn away
From the evil that he inflicts daily.

To preach the Son of God crucified
As a tragic event
For effect of rhetoric, or to persuade men
In institutions named after the Son of Man,
Is to add to the load of mankind."

"Then," I asked the elder, "Is there any hope for man
Can we be free from our own ways
Will we live forever in misery
Shall children walk the streets in despair
Wretches, worthless souls, beyond repair?
As evil walks the streets each day
Innocence is lost, although the people pray
For deliverance from the blight of death's way?"

The Elder replied,
"The Law of God is greatly to be desired
It is the law that brings man to Godly intent
The lawfulness that mankind requires
To live with his neighbor the good life
To have all good things in common
To live without misery and crime
To bring himself and his children
To freedom within, free from self-deceit
This is the Law of God,
    This is the law that Christ brings."

"Repent; turn from your evil ways
See, each day is worse, each day more woes,
Sorrows for parents, sorrows for children
Turn from your evil ways, take the easy yoke
Of common sense and common good,
Decent manners, health, vital culture.
They are at your side, in your heart,
In your lover's eyes, in the smile of your child."

"Remember the ways of Israel of old,
The Pharisees and those who by rote did hold
To the ways of hypocrisy; devoid of reason
They ate the manna from above, but all died
Stubbornly holding to their contradicted sense.
Eat the Bread from Heaven, be filled with life Divine,
Drink the water of life, be cleansed from deceit."

"You walk the street of despair,
You hear the cry of children without hope,
You groan within; the darkness has taken hold
Of your world, no-one hears, no-one turns from evil.
Why do you lose hope?
Where is your faith? Have you come to the rock
Waiting for the water to flow?
Is it your own will that thus sees
Evil continuously? Why ask the poet?
Why listen to worthless worldly wisdom?"

"Where will you find
Justice, hope, and faith,
That you need for your life?"

I replied, "Hope in this world is lacking[13]

13. Rom 8:21–24 ". . . that the creation itself will be set free from its bondage to decay and will obtain the freedom of the glory of the children of God. We know that the whole creation has been groaning in labor pains until now; and not only the creation, but we ourselves, who have the first fruits of the Spirit, groan inwardly."

Faith I cannot find in the poets verse
Justice! I strive to understand this word
In a world so indifferent to its hurt.

They are forever talking
(making the Word devoid of worth)
Of feeding the hungry, healing the sick,
Bringing hope to those born into misery,
Suicidal souls, hopelessly living each day,
Guilty of birth, fearing the light,
Seeking the night.
The well-fed, those in the public eye,
The politician and priest who willfully deceive,
Seeking public exposure
Under the pretense to bring hope
such worthless hopeless souls."

The elder said, "What then of your faith?
Your vision so divine?
The splendid destiny of mankind?
Have you also lost your hope?
What can you bring to humanity
With verse, with words, with poetry?"

I replied, "Faith can only be
From God in Heaven. It is He
That determines destiny, it is by His will
That we live, that we may be free.
I feel the pain within my soul
In verse I write a poem
This pain we all have felt
Throughout the history of man.

It was Christ who waited.
Lazarus died and was buried in the cave.
He waited, even though they prayed
He may come to heal his friend.
Mary and Martha believed that Christ

Could heal their brother,
All would not suffer.
They believed Christ their Savior.
Christ groaned within
Even as to the burial chamber he came
For their sake, so their faith may not wane.
He said, "Lazarus, come out of the cave."
Clothed in the garments of death
Lazarus walked out, to greet his friend,
To glorify God, to strengthen our faith.

Whatever deed or word
From elder or poet
It is God above who gives
Forgiveness and the peace that it brings.[14]
My verses are as your words;
An elder may through God's grace
Bring wisdom to our race,
Humanity must still choose, and by choice
In intent and deed, walk to that place
Where our savior waits."

The elder and I agreed:
The freedom of God
Is the foundation, with the cornerstone
Of the temple of the Holy Spirit
Jesus Christ
The goodness of God's glory and grace.[15]

> I saw the LORD sitting on a throne, high and lofty; and the hem of his robe filled the temple. Seraphs were in

14. Matt 11:28–30 "Come to me, all you that are weary and are carrying heavy burdens, and I will give you rest. Take my yoke upon you and learn from me; for I am gentle and humble in heart, and you will find rest for your souls. For my yoke is easy, and my burden is light."

15. Isa 28:16–17 "therefore thus says the LORD GOD, 'See, I am laying in Zion a foundation stone, a tested stone, a precious cornerstone, a sure foundation: "One who trusts will not panic." And I will make justice the line, and righteousness the plumb line.'"

> attendance . . . And one called to another and said: "Holy, holy, holy is the LORD of hosts;" . . . And he said, "Go and say to this people: 'Keep listening, but do not comprehend; keep looking, but do not understand! Make the mind of this people dull, and stop their ears, and shut their eyes, so that they may not look with their eyes, and listen with their ears, and comprehend with their minds, and turn and be healed."[16]

God has decreed
That all who have sinned
Regret the evil within.

Every man, turn from your wayward ways,
Turn from hopeless and deceitful deeds,
Turn to the Law of God.

Our streets are despair
Our future is beyond repair
Our city is cold and empty.

Say unto the stubborn,
Those born of witches curses
Who say within their hearts,
"The bricks have fallen
But we shall build with stones."

Say unto these children of hell,
"Your feasts are as the vomit of pigs
"Your days are as mad beasts
"Your foundation is the quicksand of your words
"The bricks have fallen to cover your graves
"The stones will fall to crush you in your filthy beds.

Those of the spirit of Satan
Who say, "Let us sin,
So God may grant grace,
And Christ crucified

16. Isa 6:1–10

May be justified in our sight."

The abomination of desolation
Sits on the throne of the nation,
No one fears nor cries out.
Their ways are darkness,
Death is their companion,
They conceive mischief as they bring forth wind,
Filth and vomit is without,
Evil is within.

God shall not forgive
The cruel and merciless
Who bring death
And make justice a mockery.

God does not forgive
The licentious, the unclean spirit,
The oppressor of the poor, as solemnly
They walk through the Church door;
Clothed in deeds of filth
They pray with clasped bloodstained hands.[17]

Their darkened minds
Look to the cross as a symbol
To relieve them of guilt
As they slay the innocent.

"We will solve the problems our evil brings,"
Say the hypocrite and oppressor,
While vice populates with pride,
The thief steals with an easy mind,
As the politician laughs.

> Thus says the LORD: Know that all lives are mine; . . . it is only the person who sins that shall die . . . You took your

17. 2 Pet 2:18–21 ". . . with licentious desires of the flesh they entice people who have just escaped from those who live in error . . . the last state has become worse for them than the first."

> sons and your daughters, . . . and these you sacrificed to them to be devoured. . . . You slaughtered my children and delivered them up as an offering to them.[18]

No eye has seen God
No mind has comprehended God
His goodness to life is known
By the works of his men and women

Why should the son of God die?
Why should a good man die?

We know in our hearts
As did the Pharisees
The hypocrisy within us.
We understand, better than Plato
Clearer than Aristotle,
The hatred in our hearts.
    We say we love life
Love good for our children
Husbands vow to love their wives
Wives to give birth to children of delight;
Yet do we not love the material?
Do we not value the praise of others
Above God's goodness to life?
    For 2000 years the gospels have been read
Taught in churches and schools
The great thinkers, the noble spirits
Have illuminated our minds.
    Only the Love of God
Shed abroad in our hearts
Will show us the way
The goodness to life.
    Only the Son of God
Crucified on the cross, saying,
"Forgive them father

18. Ezek 18:4; Ezek16:17–22

For they do not know what they are doing,"
Only He can remove our sins.
    Only the Holy Spirit
Can guide us and restore our reason.

This is God's revelation to us
This is the way to peace
This is the cross of salvation
    We ask for the forgiveness of our sins
We repent and embrace the Son of Man
We are embraced by our heavenly Father

By baptism in God's word, we die to sin
We receive the Holy Spirit.
This is the relationship;
Husbands love your wives
Wives love your husbands.
This is the continuation of life;
Before children are conceive
God's love is their womb.
The mother's life, as her love, flows through the child,
The father's life and love protect it from the dread.

Christ has conquered death
On the cross he defeated death
This is the life from Christ to the children of faith
It is the life of the good mother
It is the life of the loving father.

Where is the beginning?
This path so well-trodden
Rocky and narrow
It wounds past cliffs
Steep fearful depths
Towards higher hills
Lined with the caves for the dead.

I remembered; I had begun this journey

Part II

After hearing words from my folk.
They talked about love and peace,
Family, healthy children, mothers meek.
I was told on Calvary
Our savior died nailed upon a cross.
As I walked the path to Calvary
I thought I heard sounds of dismay
From shadows in the caves of death's way.

Forms seemed to move, yet I couldn't say
If they were forms or darker shadows
The sounds, weird and yet musical
Blended with the darkness abysmal.
Every sound emitted a prayer of fear,
"God of singularity, father of the primordial pit
Hear us, we pray, from thee life we seek
Our faith and hope in Darwin are complete
Our psyche is according to Freud; Oh, please heal us,
From the apes we have sprung
To glorify thine essence
You, the idea so absolute
Throughout the universe your mind we see
Hear our prayer and lift us from the abyss of death."

On the path to Calvary, coming into view
A cross on the hill ahead of me.
Above the cross, a light did appear
A figure dazzling, and I could hear the Angelic Choir.
The figure resembled my wife now with Christ.
I quickened my step
The cross did not cast a shadow
`Twas a compass to my feet
The figure from the light of heaven said,
"Death has been conquered by the lamb of God
The cross on Calvary leads
To life eternal that we seek."

As I ascended the path to the cross

The weird voices ceased their song
The shadows disappeared in the caves;
I thought a sigh exhaled from that place.

I approached the cross on Calvary
Remembering the man nailed upon it
With an inscription of being a king.
The cross that I now see
With the light from heaven above me
Shows to God's people who pray
Salvation into the life of the Way.

Standing before the cross
I received God's word:

They had covered the body with a cloth,
with tears they placed it in the cave
rolling a rock to close the entrance.
In the morning light
the women went to the cave
to shed more tears

The rock had been rolled away
The cave was empty, but the angel stayed saying,
"Why do you women mourn for him?
He has risen as he had said
Cry no more, go and rejoice at the good news."

I will ascend to heaven
After I comforted my friends
I will be sanctified
After I have strengthened their faith.

Come, feel the place where the nails tore
Talk to me, remember my words
I have thanked my Father for you all
The comforter will always be with you.

Book Three

Eternity and temporality:
I temporize as a man,
Yet in time and space
I dream beyond all limits.
I live (how?) I die (why?)
Shall I ask questions forever?

"God created all, the primal cause"
Than who created pain and death?
"God is all goodness"
Can I fathom such goodness?

Did God make a mistake in creation?
Are we free to do good?
We live by choice,
And are filled with doubt.

A philosopher and poet
Stood in awe before beauty.
"Such is the Creator's power.
Can you hear God in the bird's song?"

The philosopher perceived the universe
Felt the sand on the seashore
Slip through his hand
He sought virtue and learning, as
The stars burnt in the night
Awesome planets and galaxies!
Movement, matter, space,
Wondrous chance and chaos.

We seek God, he thought,
To escape from our ignorance.

Is it all an accident?

Beauty is all about me!
Exclaimed the poet,

Go back to your cobwebs
Or else understand goodness.

"How is the spirit of man sustained?"
Cried the philosopher
"Without knowledge we are lost."

Beauty in the sky
Beauty in the earth
Beauty in the stars
How beautiful, Oh LORD, Is your Word.

Before creation I saw her
I felt eternity shine
In her beautiful smile.

She walks in a field of tulips
Her fragrance perfumes my world.
I walk through such fields in wonder.

Before the beginning of time
God determined to call us
To be saved by the Word of God.

Even as mankind struggles with perplexity and fear
The holy seed testifies to God's grace
To those living by faith.

God freely gave the goodness of life
To those who do not bend the knee to banality
Nor are beguiled into idolatry.

> Let the heavens praise your wonders, O LORD, your faithfulness in the assembly of the holy ones. For who in the skies can be compared to the LORD? Who among the heavenly beings is like the LORD, a God feared in the council of the holy ones, great and awesome above all that are around him?[1]

The servant of God,

1. Ps 89:5–7

Met a stranger eager for the truth.

The gentile spoke:
"From my youth I have sought truth
Delighting in righteousness and wisdom
Befriending philosophers and virtuous men."

The servant of God replied, "Walk with me,
God loves those who seek the truth."

The gentile spoke of great learning:
Matter, energy, light, cosmology, epistemology,
Idealism, ultimate good, honor and duty.
His reason was splendid, his speech eloquent.

He confessed, "Knowledge is insufficient.
Thus, I have worshipped all gods
To understand the purpose of life.
Will I escape the pit of death?"

"We are saved by Jesus Christ the son of God
By the grace of the living God.
His son rose from the dead
God has poured his Holy Spirit on his children."

The stranger asked,
"What does it profit me to seek God's way of life?"

"God has granted his Holy Spirit
To those called as the first fruit
To bear witness to the revelation of his son,
God grants us his goodness, mercy, and love."

The two walked along the Way:
The stranger was eager for light
Yet his learning was a stumbling block

Humility was cultivated
Righteousness was on his works
Faith was of his intellect

He saw God in works of hands
He sought God in nature's marvels
He knew the created, but not the creator.

> O give thanks to the LORD, call on his name,
>   make known his deeds among the people!
> Sing to him, sing praises to him,
>   tell of all his wonderful works!
> Glory in his holy name
>   let the hearts of those who seek the LORD rejoice!
> Seek the LORD and his strength,
>   seek his presence continually!
> Remember the wonderful works that he has done,
>   his miracles, and his judgements he uttered,[2]

Remember how God called Moses to deliver Israel from Egypt
Though the first born of Israel were slain by the Pharaoh
God saved Moses.
Moses grew in the household of Pharaoh.

Consider the power of almighty God;
Moses grew up in the ways of sin
He was not taught the way of Jehovah by his father
His mother was not his source of virtue.

Consider the power of eternal God;
Who changed a son of the culture of Egypt
Revealing to Moses YHWH;
Moses gladly embraced rags and pain.

Ask the poet to talk of God's servants
Tell the singers to make joyful sounds to the LORD.
Re-tell the stories of His power and might
Praise God through the vessels of his Holy Spirit.

Reflect on the power of merciful God:
Many were afflicted
Struggling against injustice and pain
God's Spirit was with them

2. Ps 105:1–5

The Spirit of might comforted her
As she fought the great fight
Rejoicing in the love of God
His sacred law was written in her heart.
Comprehend the grace of the living God:
Paul of Tarsus, a Jew taught the law of Moses
Knew the law by rote as did the Pharisees
He persecuted the people of God
Throwing them in prison
Cruelly mistreating innocents
Those filled with the faith of Abraham
Obedient to the law of God
Guided by the Holy Spirit
Believing in the son of God
Reflect on the grace of God
Shown through his servant Paul
The apostle of tenderness
Who brought God's healing grace to strangers;
Paul, converted by the Holy Spirit
From a hypocritical persecutor
To live the good news of life and grace.

Tell the poet to sing of this great epic,
Order the angelic choir to assemble before the elect,
Let these words be heard in heaven,
"Rejoice oh saints of the Most High
Lift up your voices,
Sing in the presence of our God."

We walk in a world in darkness;
Our heart is filled with the light from God.[3]
We live in a world of distress;

3. 2 Cor 3:15–18 "whenever Moses is read, a veil lies over their minds; but when one turns to the LORD, the veil is removed. Now the LORD is the Spirit, and where the Spirit of the LORD is, there is freedom . . . seeing the glory of the LORD as though reflected in a mirror, are being transformed/changed into the same image from one degree of glory to another; for this comes from the LORD, the Spirit."

We are comforted by God's Spirit.
We witness the word of God despised;
While Christ was crucified for us all.
We are surrounded & overwhelmed by materialism;
We live by the grace of the living God.

As I hear the Word
I see a torrent, the blood of the slain.
As I walk on high
I hear a cry, the world in sorrow weeping.

Who shall make a sacrifice?
Who shall shed tears and sigh
For a world that is dying?

Will He accept our offering of tears?
Will He hear our prayers
As martyrs are slain before His eyes?

Our Father who is in heaven
Whose name is holy and way sacred,
Your spirit is poured on your elect
The sacred seed, for the world that rejected
Your son sent for our salvation.

As I walk on high
I see the world below
As I hear the Word
All blends into one
Love reveals the cleansing
Love gathers us into one

Will the world believe?
Oh LORD, how long will we weep?
As our tears flow freely
We eagerly seek your freedom.

By the stream of Jerusalem
We sat and ate the bread of heaven

The hills so lovely and green
Flowers decked your brow and I felt
    Heavenly bliss in your caress

By the sacred waters of life
We spoke the Word of life
The freedom of God
Paved the path we trod

By the wondrous light of your smile
We walked into the divine city.
As we passed through the gate
I held your arm and pointed above
To the treasures in our hearts,
One heart in One.

By the freedom of God
The truth that is you, my wife,
Sang the music of our faith;
"Life without end is our faith
"God shines in your face
"Our love has filled this place.

The streets of Jerusalem
Are paved with the prayers heard by God.
The gates of our city are:
Beauty in Truth
Freedom Mercy Hope Faith Joy
Forgiveness Peace Prayer
Patience Kindness Generosity

In the center of our city
No structure stands
No work is seen
One word that all see
One word that all hear
One word that all understand.

> When the day of Pentecost arrived, they were all together in one place. And suddenly there came from heaven a sound like a mighty rushing wind, and it filled the entire house where they were sitting. And divided tongues as of fire appeared to them and rested on each one of them. And they were all filled with the Holy Spirit and began to speak in other tongues as the Spirit gave them utterance.[4]

The streets of Holy Zion
Are paved with gold
Burnished by heaven's fire, purified
Thrice times thrice, our brethren in Christ[5]
Ornaments of our city Divine

At each gate a tower stands
A watcher keeps the view of our land[6]
He is asked day and night
"Watcher what do you see
"Are deceivers in our kingdom
"Is their sin in the land?

Each guard reports in his turn
"From the east I see cleanliness
"From the west happiness and bliss
"From the south the wise and the poet
"From the north the sound of lovers
God fill the four corners of the land
And it's great multitude with His Holy Spirit[7]

4. Acts2:1–4

5. Dan 11:35 "Some of the wise shall fall, so that they may be refined, purified, and cleansed, until the time of the end . . ."

Zech 13:9 "And I will put this third into the fire, refine them as one refines silver, and test them as gold is tested . . . I will say, 'They are my people'; and they will say, 'The LORD is our God.'"

6. Isa 21:8 "Then the watcher called out: 'Upon a watchtower I stand, O LORD, continually by day, and at my post I am stationed throughout the night.'"

7. Gal 5:11–26 "By contrast, the fruit of the Spirit is love, joy, peace,

Seven towers and a wall circle the city
From here the water flows into the land
Pouring like sparkling diamonds
Reflecting the light of heaven

Gardens cover the banks of the river
Flowers bloom in the field
Where golden strands of wheat
Sway in the cool breeze
Animals feed in green pasture
Surrounding the city with great bounty

The lion and the lamb
Are led by a child with golden hair
Sparkling eyes and dazzling smile
None shall hurt nor destroy
In my holy sanctuary[8]

A child's tender voice:
"I beheld a sight divine.
"A bird its wings did open wide
"It flew into the heavens so freely
"The sky unfolded its arms eagerly
"Accepted the bird with an embrace
"Then to my surprise, as if in a vision
"I beheld my mother's face

Tender Child in your Mother's gentle arms
Mary holds you in embrace
A manger she beautifies
Holy night; the star shining so bright.
Gentle Child in your Mother's tender arms

patience, kindness, generosity, faithfulness, gentleness, and self-control. There is no law against such things . . ."

8. Isa 11:5–9 "The wolf shall live with the lamb, the leopard shall lie down with the kid, the calf and the lion and the fatling together, and a little child shall lead them. . . . for the earth will be full of the knowledge of the LORD as the waters cover the sea."

Reclining on her breast,
Her peace, sweeter was this
Then the Angels song of bliss.

I hear the child singing:
"I beheld a sight so bright
"I was wrapped in her tender smile
"My mother's arms clothed me in serenity
"Security was her warm embrace

"Now before my eyes
"I see my life stretching to the sky
"Yesterdays filled with warm caresses
"Her smiling face and kisses
"Laughter from her tender eyes

Along the banks of the stream
We walked to the Holy Mount[9]
To make our vows before the LORD
Flowers marked the path we trod
Beautiful was the bird's song

I listened to your voice
I saw our children in your eyes
I drank the honey from your mouth
Eternity met us on the Way.

As we walked to the Sacred Place
The people met us on the Way
Our brothers and sisters[10]
Children running in circles

---

9. Heb 12:22–23 "But you have come to Mount Zion and to the city of the living God, the heavenly Jerusalem, and to innumerable angels in festal gathering, and to the assembly of the firstborn who are enrolled in heaven."

10. Heb 2:10–13 "It was fitting that God, for whom and through whom all things exist, in bringing many children to glory, should make the pioneer of their salvation perfect through sufferings . . . Jesus is not ashamed to call them brothers and sisters, saying . . . And again, 'Here am I and the children whom God has given me.'"

One placed a garland of flowers on your head
Because you are my bride.[11]

Is there anyone who is a devout lover of God?
Let them enjoy this beautiful bright festival!
Is there anyone who is a grateful servant?
Let them rejoice and enter into the joy of their LORD!
Are there any weary with fasting?
Let them now receive their wages!
If any have toiled from the first hour,
let them receive their due reward;
If any have come after the third hour,
Let him with gratitude join in the Feast![12]

11. Eph 5:23–33 "For the husband is the head of the wife just as Christ is the head of the church, . . . Husbands, love your wives, just as Christ loved the church and gave himself up for her, in order to make her holy by cleansing her with the washing of water by the word, so as to present the church to himself in splendor, . . . yes, so that she may be holy and without blemish . . ."

12. From the Paschal Sermon of St. John Chrysostom, read during Matins of Pascha.

The Book of Silence

Babylon the great
Worshipped Marduk, the idol of Mesopotamia.
The Hanging Gardens and the Ishtar Gate,
Formed the Processional Way for the cults.
The river Euphrates flowed through Babylon
To reflect Marduk and glorified Ishtar.
    Great empires have thus grown
To worship gods, all of them known
For the power and wealth they bestowed
To those who bend the knee.
    Egypt, unto the brightest sun god
    Athens, the glory of Athena and the pride of Zeus
(But the Athenians reserved an altar
for the god they could not know).
    Rome, the greatest city of all, built on seven hills
Worshipped idols in ceremony and pomp.

***

> At once I was in the spirit, and there in heaven stood a throne, with one seated on the throne! And the one seated there looks like jasper and carnelian, and around the throne is a rainbow that looks like an emerald. Around the throne are twenty-four thrones, and seated on the thrones are twenty-four elders, dressed in white robes, with golden crowns on their heads. Coming from the throne are flashes of lightning, and rumblings and peals of thunder, and in front of the throne burn seven flaming torches, which are the seven spirits of God; and in front of the throne there is something like a sea of glass, like crystal. Around the throne, and on each side of the throne, are four living creatures, full of eyes in front and behind.[1]

She said, "How can I believe in God

1. Rev 4:2–6

If my mother dies in pain?
All the suffering in the world;
Children starving, mothers crying,
Does God really care?"

"You have brought life into this world," I said
"You have saved the life of your child
You have shown the power of God's faith
It is God who believes in you."

Her smile was perfected
Her calm receding beneath the surface.
God poured his Spirit over her
He smiled with her smile
reminding her
His son had also died in pain.

She said to me, "I love you,"
With her perfect smile
Her wedding dress white as befits a virgin
Around her elegant neck hung
Twenty-four perfect pearls, reflecting the light
That sparkled in her eyes.

She, an innocent
I looked and my eyes could see.
She, as a child
I listened and my ears could hear.
She smiled; I saw the person,
"Come," I said, "Let us leave this world
Walk in the garden with me
Listen to the music of our souls
Talk of the poetry in our hearts."

Christ, the begotten son of God,
Before the beginning you loved us,
Beyond the end you are with us,
You are our truth, our redeemer, our Savior.

> Then God's temple in heaven was opened, and the ark of his covenant was seen within his temple; . . .
>
> A great portent appeared in heaven: a woman clothed with the sun, with the moon under her feet, and on her head a crown of twelve stars. She was pregnant and was crying out in birth pangs, in the agony of giving birth.
>
> Then another portent appeared in heaven: a great red dragon, . . . stood before the woman who was about to bear a child, so that he might devour her child as soon as it was born. And she gave birth to a son, a male child, who is to rule all the nations with a rod of iron . . .[2]

The peasants huddled in the hut
praying for darkness to cover them.
No-one dared breath
No-one dared move
In silence they prayed, "May we die."

A sound, a motor,
soldiers voices, harsh commands,
"Search each hut, drag them out,
they are enemies of the state."

They asked the child,
"Has your father betrayed the faith?"
The bewildered child looked to his mother
the bark of the soldier was clear
"Your father and mother are your enemies.

Take this gun, shoot them both
become a child of the revolution
partake of the ceremony
be baptized in the faith."

Gathered in the grove
cloaked in darkness, faces covered
they began to chant:

2. Rev 11:19—12:6

"Satan, oh Satan, goat made
to be eaten
listen to us & heed our prayer
this our potion
dedicated to thee.
You only know how we sacrificed life
& welcomed your strife
Oh, how we long for your touch
caress us
show us your power
Oh, he has come, great Satan has come . . ."

The guns ripped open the sky
The bombs shattered the earth
In the war babies were torn from the womb
And dashed against the wall.

The scientist's mind was in turmoil,
"I am like a god
I enable barren women to conceive
Yet I empower monsters,
To destroy children in their mother's womb."

We were drinking buddies
You could hardly call us friends.
But as we drank and talked
We felt like comrades.

We earnestly sought the kingdom of God
We must have been sincere!
I talked with depth
He as a true believer.

Boys trying to be men;
The world stood before us
Girls trying to be women;
Mothers of the next generation
We have the bible, we will not be deceived;

"The truth shall set us free."

I was troubled by a man dying in agony
As I watched thousands die on the TV,
Turning into a dessert, they starved, the
Matchstick women carrying the bundles of
Skin and bones born from their womb
The desert stretched into the horizon.

Where was the knowledge called pity?
Where is the awareness poets call love?
Is it found in the millions,
Who perish in pain and hopelessness?
Did they ponder the journey of souls,
While walking the path of death?

Their images will be in the information highway
We will know; we will re-defined pain.

We were so young; the world stood before our eyes.
We were so bold, the world was ready to be re-created.
We knew, we understood, we talked.

> And war broke out in heaven; Michael and his angels fought against the dragon. The dragon and his angels fought back, but they were defeated, and there was no longer any place for them in heaven.
>
> Then I heard a loud voice in heaven, proclaiming, "Now have come the salvation and the power and the kingdom of our God and the authority of his Messiah, . . . Rejoice then, you heavens and those who dwell in them!
>
> But woe to the earth and the sea, for the devil has come down to you with great wrath, because he knows that his time is short!"
>
> So when the dragon saw that he had been thrown down to the earth, he pursued the woman who had given birth to the male child . . . But the earth came to the help

> of the woman . . . Then the dragon took his stand on the sand of the seashore.[3]

"They are so perverse
They would destroy life, pervert justice
Prey on innocent children
Abuse their own flesh and blood."

"Is God helpless," I said to her
"Or can they frustrate his love?"

The Holy Spirit of God
Comforts his people,
The works of the flesh are to death
We arise, to the resurrection and the life.

"They plan theatres of war
Stockpile weapons of destruction
They pile the skulls of the slain
As their trophies of war.
They sell poisoned milk to children
Prostitute their wives for deadly narcotics!"

She and her friend cured the child
Tenderly cared for it until it walked.
She nursed the dying infant
Until it was filled with life.
The two women prayed
For another long-awaited birth.

> . . . and the temple of the tent of witness in heaven was opened, and out of the temple came the seven angels with the seven plagues . . . Then I heard a loud voice from the temple telling the seven angels, "Go and pour out on the earth the seven bowls of the wrath of God." . . . And I saw three foul spirits like frogs coming from the mouth of the dragon, from the mouth of the beast, and from the mouth of the false prophet. These are demonic spirits, performing signs, who go abroad to the kings of

3. Rev 12:7–17

> the whole world, to assemble them for battle on the great day of God the Almighty. . . . And they assembled them at the place that in Hebrew is called Armageddon. . . . The great city was split into three parts, and the cities of the nations fell . . . God remembered great Babylon and gave her the wine-cup of the fury of his wrath . . . until they cursed God for the plague of the hail, so fearful was that plague. [4]

Ho, Ariel, Ariel, city of God
Wail, wail, Oh Ariel, city of despair
Your name will be suffering
Your song will be pain.
Behold, your tormentors have arrived
They will pillage you and destroy your glory
You are no longer the city of God, oh Ariel.
For all this his anger has not turned away,
his hand is stretched out still.

The prince must divide to conquer
Total obedience is required.
The people will grow strong and prosper
As the prince great power does acquire.

A prophet spoke, "The prince desires power,
Beware oh prince, power corrupts."
The prince replied, "If the people have power
Will power corrupt not?"

Another replied, "When the morality of power
Has been shown to be lacking
A philosopher will arise amongst us
To bring reason and wisdom
The prince will embrace the good
For his people's sake
He is their protector."

What is this hypocrisy?

4. Rev 15:5—16:21

Is this a new philosophy?
Is morality found in political systems?
In democracy or in tyranny?
Will power save people's souls?

> Then I heard what seemed to be the voice of a great multitude, like the sound of many waters and like the sound of mighty thunderpeals, crying out, "Hallelujah! For the LORD our God the Almighty reigns.
>
> Then I saw heaven opened, and there was a white horse! Its rider is called Faithful and True, and in righteousness he judges and makes war. . . . From his mouth comes a sharp sword with which to strike down the nations, and he will rule them with a rod of iron; . . . On his robe and on his thigh he has a name inscribed, "King of kings and LORD of LORDS."
>
> Then I saw an angel coming down from heaven, holding in his hand the key to the bottomless pit and a great chain. He seized the dragon, that ancient serpent, who is the Devil and Satan, and bound him for a thousand years, and threw him into the pit, and locked and sealed it over him, so that he would deceive the nations no more, until the thousand years were ended.
>
> I also saw the souls . . . . . had not worshipped the beast or its image. . . . They came to life and reigned with Christ a thousand years. [5]

In Jesus Christ we have a friend
When to our neighbor we give God's blessing;
As two or three of us gather in his name
He is in our thoughts.

Jesus is our friend
When our children make joyous noises
In his celestial cathedral
He is in our hearts.

In Christ I have a friend
When my life is complex, my mind in turmoil

5. Rev 19:6—20:4

He brings peace to my heart
The blessed silence of God's name.

Jesus is our friend
When we shed tears of distress
For all of mankind's pain
He comforts us and removes the pain.

In Christ we have a friend
Come, join us in song and rejoice
He makes the unbearable bearable
He brings ease of spirit; his way is freedom.

> Then I saw a new heaven and a new earth; for the first heaven and the first earth had passed away, and the sea was no more. And I saw the holy city, the new Jerusalem, coming down out of heaven from God, prepared as a bride adorned for her husband.[6]

. . . and why will God
Wipe each tear from your eyes?
And why will he
Each cut and wound heal
As this earth and heaven pass away.

Love divine cannot die
Come my love
Within my arms repose.

With each joy, new grief we will meet
As in each other's arms we take refuge.
This day is gone so we may sleep,

The next day visits us; those moments I keep
Which bring that heavenly light
To illuminate your silky cheek.

Alas, the day also with sorrows unknown
Causes us to weep, to grieve.

6. Rev 21:1–7.

But do not talk so
Repose in my arms and sigh
Love will not argue nor strive
Even though your angry eyes strike me.

'Tis not that joy, nor tragic ways
I banish from our world;
I but believe (and you my only strength)
The wise is as the fool and the beggar as the rich
Since both do see the world around
    As love is lost to sight and sound.

You are no more,
Heaven's street is now adorned
By God's maiden who now speaks with angels

Repose in those heavenly arms
As this earth and heaven pass away
As each tear our heavenly Father wipes from your eyes
As each bruise and cut is healed with his Love divine

All things shall pass away, and we shall live anew
Within Jerusalem which God's love illuminates. . . .

> And I heard a loud voice from the throne saying, "See, the home of God is among mortals. He will dwell with them as their God; they will be his peoples, and God himself will be with them; he will wipe every tear from their eyes.
>
> And the one who was seated on the throne said, "See, I am making all things new." Also he said, "Write this, for these words are trustworthy and true."
>
> Then he said to me, "It is done! I am the Alpha and the Omega, the beginning and the end. To the thirsty I will give water as a gift from the spring of the water of life. Those who conquer will inherit these things, and I will be their God and they will be my children.[7]

It is good to praise God.

7. Rev 21:1–7

The earth longs for the word of God.
The sea roars with joy as we pray to God.

It is good to worship God.
Nations prosper and rejoice under the law of God.
Humanity is filled with glory as it obeys the will of God.

It is good to have faith in God.
Neighbor greets neighbor with the love from God.
Grace & charity are boundless; all are enriched
by the blessing of God.

It is good to be filled with the love of God.
He is life now, He is life forever, all is from everlasting God.
Ages unto ages, all nations shall raise their voices
in praises to God.

> I saw no temple in the city, for its temple is the LORD God the Almighty and the Lamb. And the city has no need of sun or moon to shine on it, for the glory of God is its light, and its lamp is the Lamb.
>
> And he said to me, "These words are trustworthy and true, for the LORD, the God of the spirits of the prophets, has sent his angel to show his servants what must soon take place. See, I am coming soon! Blessed is the one who keeps the words of the prophecy of this book."
>
> The Spirit and the bride say, "Come." And let everyone who hears say, "Come." And let everyone who is thirsty come. Let anyone who wishes take the water of life as a gift.[8]

8. Rev 21:22—22:7

Bibliography

Athanasius, St. *On the Incarnation of the Word.* Grand Rapids, MI: Christian Classics Ethereal Library. https://ccel.org/ccel/athanasius/incarnation/incarnation.i.html.

———. *Select Works and Letters.* In Nicene and Post-Nicene Fathers, Series II, Vol. 4, edited by Philip Schaff. Grand Rapids, MI: Christian Classics Ethereal Library. https://ccel.org/ccel/schaff/npnf204/npnf204.i.html.

Catholic Church. "Dei Verbum: Dogmatic Constitution on Divine Revelation." Second Vatican Council, Nov. 18, 1965. https://catholic-resources.org/ChurchDocs/DeiVerbum.htm.

Gregory of Nyssa. *Dogmatic Treatises.* In Nicene and Post-Nicene Fathers, Series II, Vol. 5, edited by Philip Schaff. Grand Rapids, MI: Christian Classics Ethereal Library. https://ccel.org/ccel/schaff/npnf205/npnf205.i.html.

John Chrysostom. "The Paschal Sermon." Orthodox Church in America. www.oca.org/fs/sermons/the-paschal-sermon.

Tanev, Stoyan. *Energy in Orthodox Theology and Physics: From Controversy to Encounter.* Eugene, OR: Pickwick, 2017.

www.ingramcontent.com/pod-product-compliance
Lightning Source LLC
LaVergne TN
LVHW020636100826
845148LV00012B/2210

* 9 7 9 8 3 8 5 2 7 3 7 2 0 *